THE CLASS STRUGGLE AND WELFARE

T0384480

The Class Struggle and Welfare

Social Policy under Capitalism

by DAVID MATTHEWS

MONTHLY REVIEW PRESS
New York

Library of Congress Cataloging-in-Publication data
available from the publisher.

ISBN 978-168590-086-1 paper
ISBN 978-168590-087-8 cloth

Typeset in Minion Pro

MONTHLY REVIEW PRESS | NEW YORK
www.monthlyreview.org

5 4 3 2 1

Contents

Acknowledgments

THERE ARE MANY PEOPLE, some of whom may not realize it, without whose support, this book would not have been possible.

I would like to extend my heartfelt thanks to Michael Yates, Erin Clermont, and everyone at MR Press. The opportunity to write this book and have it published is something I will always be grateful for. I want to thank you for your patience, enthusiasm, efforts, and good nature. The seeds of this book lie in previously published *Monthly Review* articles. Aspects of chapters 7, 8, 9 first appeared in *Monthly Review* 72, no. 8 (January 2021); *Monthly Review* 68, no. 10 (March 2017); and *Monthly Review* 69, no 4 (September 2017) respectively. Having these articles published gave me the confidence to write this book, and I am very appreciative to the *Monthly Review* editorial team for accepting and publishing them when they did.

Overt displays of affection do not come easy to me. If I were to suddenly express myself this way, those who know me well would likely be very concerned for my health. Because I don't want to cause them any unnecessary worry, they can read these words for themselves. First, Kaleb, Jacob, and Lia never make things dull. Furthermore, two recent additions to my world, Benjamin and

Isaac, are already bringing more excitement into my life. Also, I must mention my dad.

A lifelong socialist and campaigner, I want to thank my Uncle Mike who introduced me to Marx when I was fifteen. Our lengthy conversations when I was a teenager about politics and sociology were significant and stimulating and set me on a path that I am still on today. My sister Charlotte made clear how badly social change is needed to help some of the most vulnerable people in society.

I want to thank Caroline. This book would not have been written without your patience, love, and willingness to accept me disappearing and shutting myself away. This level of tolerance cannot be matched. Finally, I must thank my mum. I wouldn't have achieved anything that I have without your support and love. I have been extremely fortunate and will be forever thankful.

Introduction

CLASS CONFLICT PERMEATES CAPITALISM. The struggle between capital and labor is arguably the preeminent characteristic of all capitalist economies, the force shaping and organizing society. As Marx and Engels powerfully proclaimed in their opening to the *Communist Manifesto*, "The history of all hitherto existing society is the history of class struggles."[1] Class struggle over the means of existence, Marx and Engels asserted, was the force by which much of history was propelled and societies developed. As Engels contended after Marx's death, "It was precisely Marx who had first discovered the great law of motion of history, the law according to which all historical struggles, whether they proceed in the political, religious, philosophical or some other ideological domain, are in fact only the more or less clear expression of struggles of social classes."[2]

Class struggle penetrates all aspects of society's economic, social, political, and even scientific fields, structuring the practices and values of institutions and individuals. Class struggle implies a dialectical relationship between conflicting classes. For example, labor and capital are the two primary classes in modern capitalist societies. Because the capitalists own the means of production and the rest of us need to survive, they have great economic and political power. As a result, it might seem that they can totally dominate labor. However, "struggle" implies that labor can potentially defeat its class enemy, either temporarily or permanently. That is, the organization and operation of both the economy and society will not always reflect the interests of capital alone. The balance of class forces between capital and labor varies historically and significantly contributes to the character, organization, and operation of the economy and society. Existing capitalism, although dominated by the needs and interests of capital, is a contradictory system. Emblematic of all societies riven by the class struggle, the influence of both capital and labor is stamped upon society. Accepting the centrality of the class struggle as the organizing force of capitalist society, as this book will attempt to demonstrate, class conflict and the perpetual struggles between capital and working people must be considered as instrumental in organizing and shaping welfare state provision, both historically and continuing up to the present.

Austerity: An Expression of Class Struggle

That the organization and provision of welfare exists within a context of class conflict was epitomized in many advanced capitalist nations during the 2010s as the policies of austerity were imposed upon the populations of such countries, particularly those of Western Europe. This was fervently supported by capital and contested by labor. In Britain, responding to the growth of public debt because of the British state's expansionary fiscal measures to combat economic stagnation during the Great Financial Crisis, British governments overwhelmingly emphasized deficit reduction via a contraction of budgets. Fiscal retrenchment, specifically welfare cuts, it was asserted, were necessary to restore economic growth.[3] This agenda obtained the wholehearted endorsement of capital. The Confederation of British Industry, one of the most influential business lobbying groups in the country, urged deep cuts, except for infrastructure, while arguing any tax increases should be kept to a minimum.[4] In addition, in the spring of 2015 the then Managing Director of the International Monetary Fund, Christine Lagarde, applauded the British government's economic management.

Reductions to public expenditure and welfare provision gained the support of many among the ranks of capital, including Britain's dominant political class, along with some presumably progressive elements. It was argued that austerity was in the national interest. This reflected capital attempting to conflate capitalism's interests with the interests of the nation. However, such policies invoked fierce opposition from many among the wider population. In the first few years of the 2010s, opposition to austerity stimulated mass action in the form of protests and strikes. For example, in March 2011, 250,000 to 500,000 protesters populated London, venting their anger at public sector retrenchment. In the same year, the greatest act of industrial unrest in more than three decades took place, with over two million public sector workers, including teachers, medical professionals, civil servants, tax collectors, and librarians, withdrawing their labor in protest over below inflation wage increases, a reduction to public sector resources, and a decline in the conditions of their employment. Moreover, this was followed by one million state employees going on strike in July 2014, and an estimated 70,000–150,000 taking to the streets of London in June 2015. Then, in April 2016, over 50,000 protesters converged upon the British capital to demonstrate their opposition to nearly six years of welfare cuts.

In addition to protests and strikes, in 2013 the campaign group People's Assembly Against Austerity was launched. Supported by the labor movement, left-wing members of the Labour Party, as well as radical left parties its purpose was to organize a mass coalition against public sector and welfare retrenchment, with public displays of protest. Furthermore, the election of Jeremy Corbyn as Labour Party leader in 2015 and the growth of the left-wing Momentum movement within the party, which supported his leadership, reflected an increasing dissatisfaction with mainstream political support for austerity. Though not winning the General Election of 2017, the relatively successful performance of the Labour Party in advocating an overtly traditional social democratic agenda of public ownership, a mixed economy, increased taxes on capital, and reversing austerity policies, came as a shock for many within the dominant political class.[5]

Endorsed by capital, but encountering opposition from many within the labor force, the issue of public sector cuts and welfare retrenchment was, fundamentally, an overt expression of the class struggle. At its heart, reductions to welfare and public spending conspicuously illustrated the continuing conflict between capital and labor. Principally, capital argued that increasing public expenditure, in particular for welfare, was an impediment to capitalist expansion. But, for labor, policies of austerity reflected unconcealed attacks on living standards, economic opportunities, and the wider well-being of individuals, families, and their communities. The actions of labor—protest, strikes, and a greater receptivity to more left-wing policies—exemplified a growing class consciousness among many within the wider population. Among the working class there developed an increasing awareness of the class nature of the situation and the threat that such policies posed for exacerbating oppression, economic insecurity, and destitution. In this sense, the reactions of both capital and labor exhibited the extent to which welfare under capitalism is significantly determined by, and contextualized within, the class struggle.

Arguably, the first few years of the 2020s in Britain continued to exhibit this heightened class consciousness with welfare and public services continuing to be at the heart of this conflict. Fiscal measures implemented by the British government during the Covid pandemic to buttress capitalism—although they often benefited the working-class—reflecting interventions within the market not seen since the Second World War, were seized upon as justification to curtail public expenditures further. Reductions to public debt, made to manage inflationary pressures and aid capitalist expansion, were again asserted by capital. In response, during the period between summer 2022 and spring 2023, labor asserted itself against this renewed open attack on living standards. Teachers, nurses, paramedics, university lecturers, civil servants, postal workers, and rail workers, among others, initiated strike actions against below inflation pay deals and cuts to resources and declining working conditions, plunging the country into a prolonged wave of industrial action not experienced for decades,

Class Struggle as Central

In their effort to illustrate the relationship between capitalism and welfare, Marxist analysts, in particular some of the most influential, such as James O'Connor, Ian Gough, and Claus Offe, accepted a broadly structural account of the welfare state. They emphasized the functional advantages of welfare to enhance labor productivity, reducing the costs to capital of labor's reproduction, and promoting the ideological acceptance of capitalism within the working class. For such theorists, welfare was a mechanism to reproduce capitalism and capitalist social relations. Although many of their analyses were published over four decades ago, their functional Marxist perspective remains dominant and arguably is considered *the* Marxist understanding of welfare.[6] That the welfare state operates in a manner that supports capitalism, aiding its reproduction, is not in doubt. The concept is supported in this book, with a significant aspect of the analysis built upon this principle. That is, welfare services, for example, aid the reproduction of labor and the accumulation process. As such, many of these studies continue to remain highly relevant. However, as historical and contemporary examples from Britain illustrate, as well as throughout the advanced capitalist world over the last century, the welfare state is more than just a weapon wielded, and influenced, by capital.

As central as the concept of the class struggle is to Marxist theory, explicit reference to it to understand welfare provision is largely absent from some of the most influential Marxist perspectives of the welfare state. Previous analyses not uncommonly isolated the welfare state from the context of the class struggle. As stated clearly by welfare theorists Michael Lavalette and Gerry Mooney, "Given the centrality of class conflict and class struggle to Marxist social theory one might expect the major pieces of social welfare writing in this tradition to include a substantial account and examination of the role of class struggle in shaping welfare and social policies." However, Mooney asserts, "In the major Marxist-inspired accounts of social welfare, class, as a collective agency of social change, is . . . missing."[7] Instead, the major focus of these analyses was "the role of social policies in promoting or sustaining ideological hegemony and on the contribution of such policies to the maintenance of society." The class struggle, in particular the idea of "class as agency" whereby classes actively shape or resist welfare developments, Mooney correctly argues, was largely marginalized. Yet, for over a century, class struggle in Britain has actively determined welfare [8]

If the concept of class struggle was alluded to, not uncommonly it played only a minor analytical role with the focus, often, on class conflict from the top, instigated by capital. The role of labor in this process, and labor's contribution to the welfare state, was given scant attention. It is with reference to the working class that Lavalette and Mooney are critical of perspectives that disregard class as a collective agency of social change. That Marxist theory tends to omit labor's role within the class struggle can potentially be traced back as far as Marx and Engels themselves. Although aware of labor's struggles, political economist Michael Lebowitz argues that a failure to afford labor a central theoretical role within the analysis of capitalism is a characteristic feature of *Capital*. Lebowitz says that, aside from sporadic reference, largely relating to labor's struggle to reduce the length of the working day, "There is a fundamental problem with *Capital*—its one-sidedness. Missing from *Capital* is the side of the workers themselves."[9] "The worker is not present," Lebowitz contends, "as the subject who acts for herself against capital."[10]

The sentiments of Lebowitz pertains to previous Marxist

analyses of the welfare state. In any event, a fundamental purpose of this book is to position the class struggle as central to a Marxist understanding of welfare, and particularly to ensure that the role of the working class is recognized. Making use of historical and contemporary examples from Britain, both capital *and* labor have been vital for the initial development, evolution, and organization of the welfare state. The welfare state cannot be understood as a capitalist institution alone. As will be illustrated here, the origins of the British welfare state are firmly located in the class struggle. It was, and remains, an institution reflecting the class struggle, supporting capital's efforts to reproduce labor power and conditions of accumulation, while for labor it emerged as, and continues to be, an important means to limit exploitation and oppression. Although under capitalism welfare states are far from perfect, they offer a tentative vision of alternative values and means of organizing society.

Labor and the Welfare State

The Marxist position adopted here affords labor a prominent role. Traditionally, the labor movement has reflected reformers wishing to tame capitalism on the one hand, and more radical individuals and groups advancing the cause of socialism on the other. Historical evidence illustrates that welfare provisions were embraced throughout the labor force, often with both wings of the labor movement fighting for the same state policies. That those who have professed the desire to abolish capitalism have fought for welfare reforms, advocating policies like those supported by more reformist elements of the labor movement, reflects the recognition that reforms have always had the potential to advance the needs and values of labor without being simply compromises with capital.

Alongside insurrectionary and revolutionary tactics, advancing the cause of parliamentary reforms under capitalism has long been a weapon for Marxists. Theorists such as Lenin, Kautsky, as well as Marx and Engels, actively endorsed the establishment of reforms within the context of capitalism, as part of a wider agenda to abolish capitalism. Rosa Luxemburg, who passionately castigated those who advocated the gradual transition to socialism, and whose *Reform and Revolution* remains paramount as a call for revolutionary tactics, nonetheless recognized the value of social reforms under capitalism. With reference to the eight-hour day, Luxemburg made clear that reforms were vital as part of labor's fight, stating that the shortening of the working day was "the very least minimum of social reform which we, as representatives of the workers' interests, must demand and expect from the present state."[11] Vital for the immediate softening of labor's exploitation, social reforms, Luxemburg asserted, were essential to raise class consciousness.[12] Welfare reforms by the state have historically played a prominent role as part of a Marxist socialist reform agenda. They were pervasive within Austro-Marxism of the early twentieth century, while Lenin enthusiastically welcomed social security reforms in Russia prior to 1917. Moreover, welfare reforms were commonly supported by the Second International.

The position I adopt here is that welfare provision has the potential to challenge capitalism, both as a means of acting as a barrier against exploitation and oppression, as well as exemplifying the principles of what an alternative socialist system might be built upon. Paul Le Blanc and Michael D. Yates have discussed the Freedom Budget, a manifesto advanced by more radical members of the civil rights movement during the 1960s in the United States, in which welfare programs were central to its agenda. Although by no means an explicitly socialist program, it was advanced most effectively by socialists who viewed it as potentially aiding the transition to a democratic socialist society.[13] Reforms, although occurring within the context of capitalism, can still have revolutionary intent as they have the potential to accelerate the class struggle in the direction of socialism.

Utilized by capital as an integral mechanism to reproduce the social relations of production, but equally approved by labor as a defense against exploitation, welfare reforms curb the excess of the market system, and are symbolic of a set of values that are in opposition to commodification, individualism, competition, and oppression. The welfare state, fought for and supported by reformers and radicals alike, can be conceived as the potential nucleus of an alternative social system predicated upon altruism, community, equality, and solidarity. There exists no doubt that in its present form, and since its inception during the early twentieth century, welfare within all advanced capitalist nations exists within a capitalist context and is therefore influenced by the needs of capitalism. Yet it contains the seeds of the political economy of labor. As Lebowitz asserts, existing capitalism contains organizations, structures, institutions, and values that reflect the political economy of both capital and labor, acting as opposing forces. Institutions and mechanisms reflecting the values of labor and capital coexist under capitalism, often interpenetrating each other and subsequently shaping each other and capitalism. This latter assertion gives rise to a crucial underlying principle adopted within this analysis; that the welfare state under capitalism is a dialectical object.

Welfare as a Dialectical Object

Reflecting the assertion that the dialectical process is epitomized by constant change, capitalism has been in a state of motion since its inception. Fundamental to capitalism's transformation, as Marx and Engels wrote, has been the conflict between the opposing forces of capital and labor. The emergence of the welfare state reflected a period in the continuing evolution of capitalism as an entity (the whole), where the interaction between capital and labor (its parts), reached a point whereby the transformative conditions of capital accumulation could not be sustained in the face of the evolving conditions of oppression and exploitation experienced by labor. In the conflict of opposing forces, the welfare state developed. Indicative of the dialectic process producing something new, the emergence of the welfare state represented both the development of a new part of the capitalist whole and a contribution to the transformation of capitalism itself, from an economic system characterized by the principles of laissez-faire to a system within which the state played a greater role.

Once established, both capital and labor utilized the welfare state to pursue their own economic interests as part of the wider class struggle. Expressive of the interaction between parts of the system and the modification that can arise from this, capital and labor subsequently adapted to the emergence of the welfare state. This, in turn, influenced the gradual transformation of capital and labor and the relationship between them, namely the class struggle. Therefore, both classes experienced evolution, change, and adaptation in their acceptance and use of the welfare state during the process of class conflict, while subsequently adapting to a new capitalist environment. Additionally, the nature of the welfare state was and continues to be constituted by its role within the class struggle, and the manner in which capital and labor utilize it to advance their economic needs, with its organization and operation shaped by the class struggle.

Back to Marxism

Examining the extent to which the welfare state is a product of the class struggle, this book is firmly positioned within a Marxist theoretical framework. It will contribute to the wide body of literature regarding the welfare state, specifically by engaging with and demonstrating the relevancy of Marxism. The purpose is to illustrate the relationship between capitalism and welfare and how welfare provision is significantly determined and shaped by the rationality and contradictions of capitalism as an economic system. The pinnacle of Marxist analyses of welfare was the 1970s and early 1980s. Unquestionably, there have been important Marxist-inspired analyses of specific welfare issues since, for example, Henry Giroux on education and Howard Waitzkin's investigations of healthcare, to name but two.[14] Nevertheless, concerted efforts to theoretically interpret the wider nature of welfare from a Marxist perspective have become nearly extinct within mainstream social policy discussions, and have significantly abated as a topic of analysis within Marxist literature.[15]

Given this, I will attempt in this book to draw people's attention to the theoretical advantages and clarity that a Marxist understanding of welfare can provide. My purpose is to remind those who already embrace Marxism of the need to take seriously the welfare state as an object of theoretical analysis, to reinvigorate the subject, illustrating its relationship with capitalism, capital, and labor. Furthermore, I hope to make clear to a new generation of radical activists that Marxism is a valuable tool to aid their understanding of welfare provision, which will subsequently contribute to their wider critical body of knowledge regarding capitalism. In this sense, this book has the role of a guide, especially when it comes to those chapters that focus on specific welfare issues that illuminate a critical Marxist position of various welfare issues under capitalism. For activists, these chapters can act as a theoretical beacon informing their knowledge base.

Structure of the Book

Focusing upon state welfare, which predominates within the advanced capitalist nations as the dominant form of institutional welfare provision outside of the informal care provided by the family, chapter 1 begins with a schematic Marxist interpretation of the state. The state under capitalism is ultimately a capitalist state, having the primary purpose of enforcing and protecting the conditions of accumulation, including labor's reproduction. Yet it is also a state that, historically, reflects the class struggle, with its relative autonomy from capital providing a space for labor to influence the state's organization, such as labor's struggles for welfare. Thus, the state acts as a location for the class struggle, having the conflict between capital and labor stamped upon it, resulting in it embodying contradictory values.

Building upon chapter 1, chapter 2 continues to establish the wider theoretical context of this analysis by focusing on a Marxist understanding of welfare. This perspective will be illustrated with the works of O'Connor, Gough, and Offe encapsulating, to varying degrees, a broadly functional understanding of welfare. However, functional accounts often neglected the class struggle, in particular the role of the working class. As such, the case to consider the welfare state as a product of the class struggle, with both capital and labor influential, is made in this chapter. With respect to labor, the welfare state cannot just be understood as the domain of capital's oppression. Part of the reformist tactical tradition within Marxism, reforms, including welfare, within the context of capitalism, have historically been accepted by those wishing to overthrow capitalism. As such, a Marxist understanding of welfare cannot oversimplify the welfare state as only benefiting, and being influenced by, capital.

Chapters 3, 4, and 5 adopt a purely historical focus, illustrating the class struggle thesis of the welfare state. Although recognizing that Marx and Engels had little to say about the welfare state, largely because its development occurred after their lifetimes, an examination in chapter 3 of their perspective on factory legislation provides some indication of how both may have approached the issue of welfare. A class struggle position permeates their understanding of factory legislation, with this in turn supporting a class struggle understanding of welfare from a classical Marxist position. Focusing on Britain, chapters 4 and 5 exemplify the importance of class struggle in influencing the origins and evolution of the welfare state in the late nineteenth and early twentieth centuries. Capital's concerns regarding the relative decline of British capitalism and productivity of labor, combined with a growing awareness and fear of labor, motivated reformist elements of British capital to support the establishment of early state welfare services. Yet, while capital may have implemented these policies, capital cannot necessarily be understood as the instigator alone. A broad review of labor's attitudes to state welfare will demonstrate that the labor movement was characterized by an increasing acceptance of state welfare, as part of the class struggle, from the early twentieth century.

Chapters 6 to 10, each focus on a single welfare issue: social security, disability, health, housing, and education. The purpose of these chapters is twofold. First, a Marxist understanding of each welfare issue is presented, largely focusing on how each welfare service operates to support capitalism and the accumulation process. In this sense, this is an examination of each welfare service from the perspective of capital within the wider class struggle, and how the service supports the accumulation process. Nonetheless, furthering the class struggle thesis, a second purpose of these chapters is to illustrate, with historical and contemporary evidence from Britain, that labor has in many cases fought for these specific welfare services over the last century. And thus, while they offer advantages to capital, they have also been supported by labor to combat their exploitation and, in a few cases, to further the cause of socialism. The last chapter in the book offers a vision of a possible socialist welfare service. The foundations of such a welfare state already exist under capitalism. However, much work needs to be done to create a truly socialist provision of welfare, with some arguments presented as to what this might consist of. As well as contributing to the creation of a more equal society, a socialist welfare service will have a valuable role in a socialist society reflecting, and reinforcing, essential socialist values of altruism, collectivism, solidarity, and universalism. Central to this argument is that a socialist system of welfare, under the authority of the working-class, will have to look beyond the state. While remaining vital, the state will nevertheless need to become subservient to the authority of labor, which collectively organizes through the establishment of specifically working-class institutions.

1

Capitalism, the State, and Labor Reproduction

For Marxists, the state is an essential institution within any capitalist society, fundamental to the functioning and operation of capitalism, as it significantly contributes to facilitating the conditions of economic growth. Exactly how the state does this, and why it must act to support capitalism, has elicited varying explanations from Marxists. Yet, despite the plethora of interpretations, all are united in their agreement that the state is integral to accumulation. As urban theorist and feminist Cynthia Cockburn succinctly argued, writing in the 1970s, "The state's primary role is continually *to reproduce the conditions within which capitalist accumulation can take place*."[1] Moreover, the state under capitalism must be considered subservient to the needs of capitalism. Common to all Marxist theories of the state is to proclaim it as under the authority of capital and subordinate to capitalism.[2]

The debate as to the nature of the state has spawned a wide and often detailed literature. It is not the purpose here to engage in a comprehensive discussion of the state from a Marxist perspective. However, knowledge of it is germane to an analysis of the welfare state. An awareness of how the state operates under capitalism is invaluable in understanding how its various institutions operate, including its welfare services, which are the focus of this book.

Marxism and the State

Historically, there has probably existed no more contentious issue among Marxists than the nature of the state, in terms of its relationship with capital and labor. Acute variations of opinions abound among Marxists, and the reason for this is attributed to Marx and Engels themselves. As Bob Jessop contends, neither developed a unified theory.[3] This is because Marx and Engels's understanding of the state was historically contextualized and related to their intellectual concerns at the time; that is, they "adopted different approaches and arguments according to the problems with which they were concerned."[4] Ralph Miliband asserts that, because they never constructed a general theory of the state, understandings of what Marx thought largely developed as a result of later interpretations and adaptations.[5] Yet, as Jessop further contends, those who came after Marx and Engels, such as Lenin, Trotsky, and Gramsci, although providing acute observations, largely failed to provide a complete theoretical exposition of the state and its relationship to the process of accumulation.[6]

Although recognizing the complexity of this issue, Miliband identifies four core functions of the state under capitalism. First, the maintenance of social order via repressive methods; second, a means of obtaining consent from the population as part of the state's ideological operation; third, promotion of what is considered to be in the "national interest"; and finally, ensuring an environment conducive to the expansion of capitalism.[7] Aside from the detail of its specific functions, the primary role of the state under capitalism is to defend and support the capitalist economy "upon whose health (or lack of it)," as Vicente Navarro insisted, "everything else is assumed to depend," including the health of the state itself.[8] For capitalism to be reproduced as an economic system, fundamental conditions that facilitate accumulation must be protected. The state, Miliband writes, sustains capitalism "in a multitude of different ways," primarily doing so "in accordance with 'rationality' of the capitalist mode of production."[9]

Famously, in the *Communist Manifesto* Marx and Engels stated: "The executive of the modern State is but a committee for managing the common affairs of the whole bourgeoisie."[10] Here they were asserting that the state is an apparatus utilized by capital to ensure that the conditions necessary for accumulation are maintained. The state as an instrument of capital is a theme that, although subject to refinement, frequently appeared within the works of Marx and Engels.[11] This perspective pervaded Lenin's conceptualization, and the notion of it as a coercive institution specifically characterized his interpretation. For Lenin, the state was a repressive instrument of social control, an apparatus of bourgeois repression; he argued that "the state is a machine for maintaining the rule of one class over another."[12] Drawing upon Engels's assertion that the state is characterized by armed organizations and institutions of coercion utilized to maintain the exploitation of the oppressed class, Lenin drew attention to the existence of "special bodies of armed men" tasked with forcibly imposing the authority of capital upon labor.[13] In a similar vein, Louis Althusser understood the state as ultimately a repressive apparatus. "The Marxist-Leninist 'theory' of the State has its finger on the essential point," Althusser said, with repression epitomizing its essential function.[14]

The conceptualization of the state as an instrument in the hands of capital was seized upon by Paul Sweezy. For him, the state has the fundamental purpose of enforcing and maintaining capitalist property relations and ensuring the perpetuation of the economic and social structures from which capital and labor arise as competing classes. As he asserted, the state "is the product of a long and arduous struggle in which the class which occupies what is for the time the key positions in the process of production . . . will enforce that set of property relations which is in its own interest."[15] In a position of economic authority, having at its disposal the means of production, the state will ultimately act in the interests of capital, as capital's economic dominance ensures that it compels the state to maintain the economic organization from which its authority over labor is based. As such, the state has the primary function of protecting all that contributes to the prevailing class structure under capitalism, the continuing subservience of labor to capital, capital's continuing ownership of the means of production, and thus, ultimately, capitalism. On this basis, building upon Marx and Engels's own assertion, Sweezy conceives the state as "an instrument in the hands of the ruling classes for enforcing and guaranteeing the stability of the class structure itself."[16] It is thus the primary responsibility of the state, through legislation and force, to conserve the conditions that allow for the continuation of capitalism, and, more specifically, an environment conducive to accumulation and surplus value production.

The State and Class Conflict

Given that it is integral to the maintenance of capitalism and surplus value production, the state occupies a prominent role as an instrument of class domination and is thus central to the class struggle. That the state can be understood as operating for the benefit of capital can in large part be attributed to its historical evolution, developing in response to the emergence of private property. Drawing upon dominant anthropological data at the time of his writing, Engels asserted that the state emerged as the first recognizable form of developed human society, starting with the growth of Athenian society. Unlike earlier epochs, which were characterized by collective ownership of the means of production and cooperative social relationships, the state, with the growth of modes of production based upon private property, evolved as an institution to contain emerging class antagonisms.[17] As such, the state is rooted within the material conditions of a society based upon exploitative production and private property, and it emerged as a consequence of the need to protect this system and facilitate its continuation. Not only is the state largely presided over by those representing the interests of property in this economic structure, but it operates to reinforce class relations. Its very existence is determined by, and predicated upon, being part of a society characterized by oppression and exploitation .

It is vitally important, however, not to conceive of the state as solely an instrument of capital. The class struggle is one fought both directly and indirectly, not just by capital, but by labor as well. And while within any capitalist society, the state remains first and foremost an instrument of capital's oppression, this in no way means, as history proves, that the state cannot act in the interests or reflect the values of labor if the political, economic, and social conditions allow. As tempting as it is to consider political and social institutions as only instruments of capital, history contends that many of the same institutions capital has utilized in its efforts to support the process of surplus value creation have also been embraced by labor to assert itself and resist exploitation.

The class struggle is inscribed on the capitalist state, reflecting in its organization and operation the antagonism between capital and labor. The extent to which the authority of one dominates the other in any given socioeconomic historical moment influences its character and nature. The state reflects the current balance of power between labor and capital. Moreover, it reflects specific historical moments, events, and periods in which the balance of class power mirrored the authority of either capital or labor. For instance, the state's form and organization at a point in time can reflect historical moments when the authority of labor was great, even though currently that of capital may have been enhanced. That is, historical moments within the class struggle may remain captured within the present organizational form of the state. For example, the continuing existence of the British National Health Service more than seventy years after its inception exemplifies the solidification and institutionalization of a moment when labor had influence over the organization of the British state.

That the class struggle significantly shapes the organization of the state is embedded in the works of Marx and Engels. Miliband observes that "the idea that class struggle is of decisive importance in determining the nature and form of the state is a familiar part of classical Marxism."[18] While never disputing that the state under capitalism has the fundamental purpose of protecting capitalist property relations and ensuring an environment for expanded accumulation, the nature of the state, Miliband asserts, is greatly determined by the class struggle and the extent to which labor can challenge the hegemonic influence of capital.[19] In practical terms, real differences exist between varying nation-states because of current and historical class struggles within those countries. This gives rise to such differences as those between states identified as social democratic in nature and those that reflect liberal capitalist values. Although both are capitalist, with their underlying structures conforming to the rationality of capitalism, their difference in organization and policies reflects current and historical variations in the balance of class power between capital and labor.

Accepting that states reflect the class struggle, it can subsequently be asserted, as Miliband does, that political and social organizations, instead of being mere instruments of capital, can be arenas and sites of class conflict fought over by both capital and labor.[20] Mirroring the balance of class forces, many institutions are frequently contradictory in nature, organized and operating in a way that is simultaneously illustrative of capital's interests *and* the struggles fought by labor. As potential arenas of class conflict, institutions can act to solidify the dominance of capital, but, equally, they can act as locations through which labor attempts to combat its exploitation and enhance its own reproduction. Miliband's position revolves around the notion that the state and its institutions have the potential to develop and operate dialectically, caught within the class struggle, with their organization and operation determined by the continuous advancement and altering circumstances of the class struggle between capital and labor, with both attempting to influence the state's actions, utilizing and benefiting from the same state institutions as a means of advancing their own class interests.

Rather than a static object always operating for the benefit of capital, the state is instead characterized by a degree of flexibility. It is as an evolutionary institution reflecting the historic nature of the social and economic relations of capitalism and the actions of classes. The state, as Cockburn contended, must be considered as specific to both time and place.[21] In a similar vein, for Philip Corrigan, Harvie Ramsay, and Derek Sayer, the nature of any capitalist state must be viewed as determined by "the social relations and conditions of specific modes of production *in their historical development*."[22] The relations between labor and capital permeate the organizational form and operation of the state at any one point in history. As a result, it should not be understood as fixed. Instead, it is relatively fluid, reflecting changing patterns of relationships between social classes and the class struggle.[23] Consequently, rather than discuss the state abstractly, it must instead be understood in terms of state *forms*, as an institution whose nature and organization is historically determined depending upon the nature of the class struggle. In a dialectical sense, it is an object in constant motion because of the forces of class struggle acting upon it.

Engels: The State as an Object of Class Struggle

That there exists an immediate relationship between the state and class struggle was asserted by Engels. The state is a "product of society at a certain stage of development; it is the admission that this society has become entangled in an insoluble contradiction with itself."[24] This is the contradiction of class conflict. Engels posited that in a society divided between classes based upon production, the state will always be presided over by the economically dominant. First and foremost, the state is an oppressor. It is "the state of the most powerful, economically dominant class, which . . . becomes also the politically dominant class."[25] Moreover, the state is "in all cases . . . essentially a machine for keeping down the oppressed and exploited class."[26]

To combat the contradiction of class conflict, the state must act "in order that these antagonisms . . . might not consume themselves and society in a sterile struggle," with the state becoming "a power seemingly standing above society . . . necessary for the purpose of moderating the conflict."[27] The state should be considered a product of class struggle. Its very existence develops from the opposing forces of a class of exploiters and a class of the oppressed, with the state a necessity to contain economic struggle between the two. Yet Engels said that specific historical moments may result in the conflict between exploiter and oppressed reaching an impasse. During such periods the state assumes a position of an authority situated above the class struggle, acting as an arbitrator in the conflict to protect the long-term interests of the dominant class.[28] The seeds of this position can be identified as characterizing some of Marx's own statements. Although certainly never rejecting the notion of the state dominated by and acting in the interests of capital, Marx, Miliband contends, also recognized periods when the state may assume the role of independent from, and superior to, all social classes.[29]

For Engels the state is not simply an instrument in the possession of the exploiters, solely reflecting their dominance. There exist moments when the authority over the state by the economically dominant is tempered, when the conflict between exploiter and oppressed reaches a deadlock. A balance of class forces results in the state assuming a role of mediator between both classes, with the state assuming a degree of autonomy from both. "By way of exception," Engels asserted, "periods occur in which warring classes balance each other so nearly that the state power, as ostensible mediator, acquires, for the moment, a certain degree of independence from both."[30] Building upon this, some later Marxists took this position one step further, explicitly stating that there are moments when labor can influence the organization and structure of the state.

For social work theorists Philip Corrigan and Peter Leonard, the state "reflects the balance of class forces . . . sometimes it reflects the overwhelming dominance of one class and at other times a more closely balanced set of class forces."[31] Additionally, as housing academic Sean Damer pointed out, the state is the "cockpit of class struggle," with its structure "the outcome, the expression, of class struggle."[32] The state, therefore, should be considered an evolving organizational form. This evolution, however, is not in a linear deterministic manner progressing from one stage to another. Rather, it reflects the dialectical process, a fluid organizational development echoing the contestations of the class struggle under capitalism and the balance of class forces at any given moment. The state is constituted by the class struggle, from both above and below, with the authority of both classes reflected at any time, depending upon the historical, political, and social circumstances. As Damer claimed, "According to specific historical conditions, different balances of class forces and patterns of class alliances will characterise different periods of the social formation, and will be reflected in the apparatuses of the state."[33] Under capitalism the state is a class struggle state. For welfare theorist Jennifer Dale, writing in the early 1980s, the state is an expression of class power, with its structure and functioning determined, on the one hand, by capital's attempt to reproduce its dominance, and, on the other, labor's efforts to combat its exploitation.[34] Consequently, the capitalist state cannot simply be viewed as operating only for the benefit, and in the interests, of capital. Rather, it exhibits contradictory tendencies determined by the class struggle.[35]

Relative Autonomy of the State

Asserting, as both Marx and Engels do, that the state can assume a position of some independence, gives rise to the notion that the capitalist state has a degree of autonomy. Again, Miliband states this with clarity: "All states enjoy some autonomy or independence ... from all classes, including the dominant classes."[36] The purpose of this autonomy is to ensure the state has a degree of flexibility to act in ways considered best to contain the class struggle and strengthen the long-term interests of capital as a whole, rather than acting in the short-term interests of some, although moments can arise when a fraction of capital may dominate the state over other capitalist groupings. This independence, far from reducing the class nature of the state, reinforces it. Its autonomy, Miliband says, helps "to explain a crucial attribute of the state in capitalist society, namely its capacity to act as an agency of reform."[37]

For Sweezy, it was fundamental for the state to ensure there existed little impediment to capitalism's operation because it was a vital economic instrument. As a result it had the responsibility of intervening within both the economy and society, by whatever means necessary, to modify and eliminate any obstructions and barriers restricting capitalism's operation.[38] Penetrating to the heart of capitalism, an irreversible contradiction that forever plagues the economic system, is the antagonistic relationship between capital and labor, with this conflict commonly stimulating the state to intervene on behalf of capital to ensure class relations are preserved. Of importance in this process is the state's willingness to provide concessions to labor, which, even if not obviously in the interests of capital in the short term, are nonetheless in its interests in the long term, as this will support the continued preservation of capitalism.[39]

While the state's autonomy is essential for it to act in the interests of capital, this degree of autonomy allows labor to influence the operation of the state during particular periods. Labor has been historically successful in gaining victories and winning concessions from capital that in turn influence the operation of the state.[40] In the need to contain the class struggle, under pressure and at times expressing fear, capital has utilized the state to bequeath concessions to labor. As welfare academic Caroline Bedale argued, "There can be significant shifts in the relative positions of capital and labour even while the capitalist system remains."[41] The result, as Corrigan and Leonard correctly posited, is that in the short term the class struggle between capital and labor can, under

certain circumstances and conditions, have the consequences of
the state acting against the interests of capital.[42]

Though it is essential that the state acts in the interests of capital, its autonomy nonetheless presents capital with a challenge,
as it affords labor the opportunity to fight for and claim victories
that are in opposition to capital. The state subsequently acts as a
space for labor to assert itself and challenge its position. Because
the state's autonomy is vital for capital to maintain social stability, it introduces social reforms that it hopes will placate labor.
However, it risks allowing labor the opportunity to challenge capital's authority, using, and building upon, reforms to chip away at
capitalism, even if not threatening it entirely. Labor is able to influence the state to implement reforms and policies, such as welfare
measures, that reflect the values of labor and contradict those of
capital. Combined with extra-parliamentary activities, such as
direct action along with conscious-raising efforts, the influence of
labor on the policies and actions of the state can potentially contribute to broader efforts to challenge the capitalist system.

It is within this context of a capitalist state reflecting the nature
of the class struggle, with capital utilizing the state to offer reforms
to placate labor, but labor adopting the state and reforms as crucial
for it as part of the class struggle, that we can begin to understand
the role of state welfare services. Although potentially effective
in counteracting labor's threat, the creation and establishment of
state welfare services have the potential to embed within the state's
apparatus, and within wider society, working-class values of collectivism, solidarity, universalism, and decommodification. These
values are in opposition to capitalist values of individualism, competition, self-reliance, and the commodity principle. The state can
subsequently become a space under capitalism that displays in its
organization and operation competing values, as the state's autonomy can result in the institutionalization of working-class values
alongside capitalist values because of labor taking advantage of the
state's autonomy and influencing the direction of reforms implemented by capital.

Competing Systems and Values

Michael Lebowitz professes that capitalism is a contradictory system comprising values and institutions that are in opposition to capital. Capitalism contains institutions, organizations, practices, and values of an alternative system, one that reflects the political economy of the working class. As Lebowitz argues, "The political economy of capital versus the political economy of the working-class—these are sides of the class struggle within existing capitalism."[43] The nature of "really existing" capitalism is that it can contain and exhibit the seeds and foundations of an alternative system upon which economic and social life could potentially be organized, given that there may already exist institutions under capitalism that make more likely the creation of this new system, while capital still predominates. These foundations of an alternative to capitalism are, Lebowitz says, "alien to the organic system of capitalism."[44]

Reflecting the dialectical process, the values of capital and labor coexist under capitalism, interpenetrating, which subsequently impact their respective natures. As such, neither capital nor labor exists in a "pure" state; rather, each is transformed by its interaction with the other. Opposition and conflict between these two classes can be considered as contested reproduction. In this struggle, the state plays an instrumental role, with the struggle over the state one between two opposing systems of political economy. As Lebowitz further argues, "In contested reproduction . . . the state is a site of struggle, to determine whether and to what extent it serves to support the reproduction of capitalism or the society of associated producers."[45]

Offering a similar position, sociologist Erik Olin Wright asserts that the capitalist state, while operating in favor of capitalism, can simultaneously reflect the values of labor. Existing capitalist systems, Wright proposes, are an amalgamation of both capitalist and non-capitalist relations, and though capitalist values predominate, there are spaces that reflect anti-capitalist values. The capitalist state, Wright says, should be understood within this vein. Capitalist states are complex, exhibiting both capitalist and anti-capitalist values and institutions. This complexity has its origins in the fact that the actual nature of the capitalist state, in its organization and operation, is determined by the class struggle. Wright states that "the trajectory of compromises and concessions, victories and defeats, is thus registered in both the formal design and informal norms within political institutions."[46]

The contradictory nature of the capitalist state, and its ability to reflect and be influenced by capitalist and working-class values simultaneously, can be exemplified by social democracy. Accepting that social democracy strengthened capitalism, especially in the immediate postwar era, and was in no way a means of offering the initial stages on the road to socialism, it is, nonetheless, the case that social democracy "expanded the space for various socialist elements in the economic ecosystem."[47] State provision of services and decommodification offered spaces beyond the sphere of the market, exemplifying broad alternatives and foundational principles upon which opposing means and methods of action to capitalism could be based. Although supporting capitalism, it would be quite wrong, Wright says, to suggest that there was nothing anti-capitalist about the state's actions, particularly the policies of social democracy. "It is entirely possible for a form of state intervention to have the immediate effect of solving problems for capitalism, and even strengthening it, and nevertheless set in motion dynamics that have the potential to erode the dominance of capitalism over time."[48]

It is in this sense that the welfare state can be understood. As part of the capitalist state, it is influenced in its origins, organization, and operation by the needs of capital. But, as an institution, it also reflects an alternative system, as it exhibits values largely in opposition to those of the market. Many welfare services present the basis of a system established upon values of universalism, collectivism, altruism, and providing for all based upon need and inability to pay. Yet, existing with the system of capital, the principles of the market have penetrated the welfare system, perverting its radical potential and subsequently influencing it to act in the interests of capital. Nonetheless, it embodies the basis of an alternative system, which, under the direct authority of labor, could oppose capital and capitalist social relations. It is this understanding that contextualizes much of the historical evidence presented in this analysis of labor's struggles for welfare.

The State and the Reproduction of Labor

A central tenet of the class struggle for capital is labor's reproduction. The reproduction of labor, according to Marx, was essential for renewing the conditions of production and ensuring the viability of continuous and future accumulation.[49] Moreover, as Cynthia Cockburn has made clear, "The capacity of men and women to work is the most important productive force."[50] Reproduction of labor power has been, as it continues to be, a fundamental arena of class conflict. Within the context of the class struggle, the state is integral. However, it is essential that a one-dimensional understanding of the relationship between the state and the reproduction of labor is avoided. As already noted, under capitalism the state is an institution reflecting to varying degrees the balance of class forces. Acceptance of the state as a dialectical phenomenon during the reproduction of labor, shaped by capital *and* labor, is crucial.

The process of reproducing labor power permeates the operation of the welfare state under capitalism, and it is this reproduction, and its necessity, that infuses the class struggle and propels it, with both capital and labor seizing upon welfare as a mechanism to support the process. For capital, conscious of the imperative need to have a pool of labor of sufficient quality for the maintenance of capitalism, welfare services, even if publicly lamented, are largely accepted as integral to the process of producing a labor force with the capacity to be exploited profitably. Individual units of capital, it is recognized, do not have the capacity, resources—both financial and organizational—nor the inclination to contribute significantly to labor's reproduction outside of providing wages. As such, despite ideological objections to a greater role for the state in society, practicality of circumstances has meant that in reality capital has pragmatically conceded the need for the socialization of many of labor's reproduction costs. This concession has been made easier by the fact that socialization of costs is ultimately of economic advantage to capital in terms of being cheaper than if labor's reproduction was directly financed. It is for these reasons, as history illustrates, that capital has accepted welfare reforms, albeit constantly attempting to influence them so that they satisfy the needs of capital as much as possible.

Furthermore, labor's reproduction has been of significance for many within its ranks. As conducive as labor's reproduction is to capital, the state institutions that contribute to this are essential from the perspective of labor for its own reproduction and are frequently accepted by labor and defended during periods of threat. Despite their paltry nature, in many advanced capitalist nations state welfare services are recognized by labor as essential to the maintenance and reproduction of many within society. Although barriers to social mobility in the advanced capitalist nations remain rigid, a universal system of compulsory education and expansion of tertiary institutions has without doubt strengthened labor's opportunities. While frugal, existing social security for families vitally enhances family budgets, especially in an era of stagnating wages. Similarly, it offers a modestly reduced threat of destitution, particularly for those unable to work due to sickness, long-term illness, and disability. Moreover, a public healthcare system does ensure that the financial costs of poor health are collectively met by society.[51] As Cockburn stated, it is essential not to consider the state's welfare provision as beneficial for capital or even bequeathed to labor by capital. But instead, in many incidences, these provisions were won by labor within a context of oppression as institutions aiding labor's fight against exploitation. "In this respect," Cockburn writes, "the welfare state was a *real* gain for the working class."[52]

Although the state has the fundamental purpose of protecting and supporting surplus value creation, and the conditions of exploitation upon which this is predicated, it is also a class struggle state, reflecting the balance of class forces. History exemplifies that during the class struggle the state has acted in the interests of labor as well as capital. The instruments and services of the state have been utilized to pursue the interests of both capital and labor, and thus adopt a contradictory character in that they do not always operate for the advantage of one class over another. This characterizes the state's welfare services under advanced capitalism. Any Marxist conception of welfare must acknowledge the dialectical nature of welfare services as being fundamentally part of a state apparatus whose character and nature is determined within the context of class struggle. For sure, welfare services under capitalism are essential for capital to continue to impose its dominance and support the reproduction of the conditions of production, especially labor power. But, despite their often punitive nature and limited generosity, these are vital services, embraced by labor in recognition of their importance to their physical and mental well-being, which is crucial to mitigating the consequences of an existence underpinned by exploitation and oppression.

—— 2 ——

Marxism and Welfare

Marxist analyses of the welfare state reached their zenith during the 1970s and early 1980s. Among the publications of this era, the most compelling were those of James O'Connor, Ian Gough, Norman Ginsburg, and Claus Offe.[1] Additionally, this period spawned a number of significant analyses of specific welfare issues, including social work, healthcare, education, and old age.[2] From these investigations, varying competing Marxist understandings emerged, with the welfare state portrayed as an essential means via which capital imposes social control upon labor, crucial to continued surplus value production, or, in opposition to this, as incompatible with capitalism, as well as the embodiment of socialist principles within market societies.[3]

Of all interpretations, that welfare has the purpose of maintaining and reproducing the conditions of accumulation has dominated Marxist analysis. Common to many Marxist investigations of welfare is the dominance of what we can describe as a broad functionalist paradigm that examines how welfare serves the "needs of capital"[4] In the process, as British social policy theorist Kirk Mann contends, there emerged a neglect of the subjects of social policy, particularly the poor and the labor movement. Mann also asks what happened to the class struggle in these analyses. Although not ignoring it altogether, the focus upon functionalist concerns meant, as social work activists Michael Lavalette and Gerry Mooney argue, that despite the centrality of class struggle within Marxist theory, the role of class in shaping welfare was largely absent from these investigations.[5]

Function of Welfare

To understand how Marxists have perceived the welfare state as serving the needs of capital, an apprehension of the positions of O'Connor, Gough, and Offe is essential. For O'Connor, the state is responsible for maintaining the conditions of profitability and social harmony: "The capitalist state must try to fulfill two basic and often contradictory functions—*accumulation* and *legitimization*."[6] O'Connor identifies two forms of state outlays that help to achieve these goals. The first, social capital expenditure, is crucial to supporting capital accumulation and can be divided between social investment expenditure, used to enhance the productivity of labor, and social consumption expenditure, utilized to reduce the costs of reproducing the labor force. Social investment spending can include investment in physical capital such as roads, railways, and utilities, services that capital requires on a permanent basis, and human capital, of which education is central.[7] Similarly, social consumption spending includes expenditure on services and facilities collectively consumed by the labor force that contributes to the reproduction of labor power, including roads, schools, hospitals, and childcare services, as well as social security provisions, such as unemployment, pensions, and sickness benefits.[8]

To maintain social harmony, the second main form of state outlay is that of social expenses. Welfare services contribute to a sense of security and fairness among workers. This goes some way toward mitigating class struggles and subsequently protecting capitalism. In this sense welfare services adopt a crucial ideological role, as their very existence attempts to confer upon labor an understanding of capitalism as benevolent. Therefore, O'Connor understands the welfare state to have a vital social control function. It is a mechanism that attempts to regulate behavior and contribute to the wider process of socialization.

The needs of capitalism are also fundamental for Gough. The welfare state, Gough argued, should be understood as "the use of state power to modify the reproduction of labour power and maintain the non-working population in capitalist societies."[9] The reproduction of labor power is a preeminent function of the welfare state. Through taxation and social security programs, the welfare state can regulate the amount individuals have to spend on use values. Moreover, it can subsidize those goods and services whose use values are essential for labor power, such as housing or food. Additionally, it can directly provide goods and services, entirely for free or at a greatly reduced charge, which are essential for labor's reproduction, such as health and education.[10] Furthermore, while identifying the material and physical reproduction of labor, Gough, like O'Connor before him, also identified the welfare state's ideological role. Education and social work services, Gough contended, were crucial to the socialization process, attempting to instill in individuals acceptable attitudes and forms of behavior beneficial to capitalism.[11]

Alongside the reproduction of labor, the second core function of the welfare state, Gough made clear, was the maintenance of non-laboring groups. Society contains individuals such as children, the elderly, individuals with disabilities, the long-term sick, those with caring responsibilities, and the unemployed who are not part of the labor market. Therefore, mechanisms must be put in place to ensure their material existence. Although the family, and to a certain extent the wider community, as well as charities and voluntary organizations, remain important to this process, the welfare state plays a vital role. Social security is central, providing a minimal level of income. Though not part of the labor force, many in these groups are likely to become members in the future, such as children as well as those who are unemployed. Consequently, the welfare state has the function of maintaining the labor power of future members of the labor force. Subsequently, the two core functions of the welfare state identified by Gough are inextricably linked.[12]

Similar to the analyses of both O'Connor and Gough, Offe's analysis has significantly shaped Marxist understandings of welfare. Capitalism, Offe said, exhibits a tendency to evolve toward a crisis of accumulation: "The key problem of capitalist societies is the fact that the dynamics of capitalist development seem to exhibit a constant tendency to *paralyse* the commodity form of value."[13] Mitigating such a crisis, the state must actively intervene. This intervention should be understood as "administrative recommodification."[14] To protect the accumulation of capital, the state cannot intervene directly within the economy, as this would threaten the principle of the commodity form. Instead, the state must intervene indirectly through the provision of various services. For Offe, attention must be directed toward supporting the demand for, and consumption of, both capital and manufactured goods, as well as enhancing the productivity of labor power. With regard to the latter, public infrastructure investment is considered crucial, including investment in education, being essential to enhancing the productivity of labor, but also reproducing it. It is here where Offe specifically identifies services commonly associated with the welfare state.[15]

Labor Struggles and Welfare

Proclaiming that the welfare state serves the needs of capitalism is an integral characteristic of any Marxist position. Indeed, it forms an integral aspect of this analysis. The criticism, however, is that many of the most influential Marxist analyses, while correctly identifying the functional qualities of the welfare state, largely fail to adequately situate this analytical position within the context of class struggle. Primarily focusing on the needs of capitalism results in the objectification of the welfare state. It has been evaluated abstractly, characterized as a component within a wider but integrated economic and social structure, illustrating its functional qualities for the operation, maintenance, and reproduction of that structure, but failing to acknowledge it as a product of class struggle. Additionally, the dominant Marxist conception, even if acknowledging the role of class conflict, often recognizes only the role of capital. This offers a one-sided understanding, as it ignores the significant historic contributions made by the working class to the development of the welfare state. That welfare is the product of class struggle was asserted by sociologist Vicente Navarro. Yet he contended that class struggle, as a determining factor, had been largely absent from efforts to explain the nature, character, and timing of social legislation.[16] This is still true today. For Navarro, the growth of welfare services, throughout the advanced capitalist nations, should be considered as inextricably related to the class struggle, with both capital and labor instrumental to the expansion of the welfare state. And it is this concept that will be supported and advanced here.

Eschewing the class struggle fails to consider the welfare state as a dialectical phenomenon. The state, in the last instance, is ultimately under the authority and influence of the economically dominant class. Yet to contain the class struggle a degree of autonomy must exist between capital and the state to serve the long-term interests of capital. It is this degree of autonomy that provides the room and opportunity for labor to influence the operation of the state to varying degrees, including the welfare state. Subsequently, though the state and the welfare state are institutions operating for the benefit of capitalism in the long term, and can be described as capitalist institutions, autonomy from the direct control of capital means that the welfare state can be influenced by, and reflect the values and strength of, labor. The welfare state, then, is a capitalist institution but reflects the class struggle.

It is on this basis that we can understand the welfare state as a dialectical object. The degree of autonomy afforded the state allows it, and many of its institutions, including the welfare state, to become arenas of class conflict, utilized by both capital and labor in order to assert their own needs. In the process, the welfare state can come to reflect the interests of both classes. Class struggle is instrumental in influencing the organization and operation of the welfare state. As Marxist-inspired social work theorists Ian Fergusson, Michael Lavalette, and Gerry Mooney assert, welfare "settlements" take a variety of forms within all capitalist nations, illustrative of the fact that the organization, structure, and character of any welfare state cannot simply be reduced to the accumulation needs of capitalism alone. Wider social and political forces are also significant, including the class struggle, that is, the relationship between capital and labor.[17]

Welfare and Forces from Below

Although not featured prominently within the literature, there has been an attempt by some to embed the concept of class struggle within their analysis of the welfare state. One such effort was by the New Left historian John Saville. The British welfare state, Saville contended, emerged from within the framework of the class struggle.[18] Anticipating the arguments of later Marxists, Saville states that the changing needs of capitalism influenced the development of the British welfare state, in particular encouraging greater productivity from labor. The growth of welfare provision was thus, in part, driven by the need to enhance the conditions of labor's reproduction to ensure productivity.[19]

Much of Saville's argument concentrates on determining the influences of capital and labor upon the evolution of welfare: "The Welfare state . . . has come about as a result of . . . the struggle of the working class against their exploitation," along with "recognition by the property owners of the price that has to be paid for political security."[20] For Saville, integral to the development and expansion of welfare provision in Britain were the political calculations of ruling groups to maintain their authority, in addition to the irresistible pressures coming from labor.[21]

Labor's contribution to the creation of the British welfare state, Saville believed, was not in doubt. Stating his position succinctly, he claimed "the pace and tempo of social reform have been determined by the struggle of working-class groups and organisation."[22] While accepting the influence of capital, he asserted that there appeared to be a degree of influence upon the construction of the welfare state by labor that surpassed that of capital. It was not "the middle class or any group of property owners who have been the prime movers in social change." Nor is it "the abstract calculation of enlightened self-interest on the part of the great employer or the vigorous conscience of a minority of middle class humanitarians."[23] Rejecting the notion that capital primarily shaped the establishment of welfare in Britain, Saville asserted that, ultimately, the most significant "determining factors in the evolution of the Welfare state will be the degree of organisation and determination to insist upon change, on the part of the working people themselves." This determination was expressed in "the massive development of the working-class movement and the recourse to methods of direct action," which had been "able to shift mountains of unreason that have built themselves upon the foundations of private property."[24] The implementation of welfare measures was, therefore, significantly determined by the presence and demands of the working class.

Writing in response to Saville, and objecting to a perceived understating of the significance of the working class in his work, historian Dorothy Thompson asserted vigorously that the welfare state was more than just a gift bequeathed to labor by capital. Analyzing the British welfare state in the 1950s, Thompson noted that many of its services were provided based on need, with no monetary transaction involved. For her, this was fundamentally an anti-capitalist principle. It was the outcome of struggle, for which labor continuously fought. Support for welfare services, Thompson wrote, "has always come from the organised labour movement. . . . What is more, the opposition has always come from the spokesmen of property."[25] For Thompson, the labor movement had been integral to the establishment of welfare, with the welfare state representing a victory for the working class.

Because state welfare services were provided on the basis of need and not the ability to pay, their significance, Thompson claimed, "is that these are, objectively, victories for working-class values within capitalist society."[26] She understood state welfare services as reflecting socialist principles and ambitions, with it perfectly possible that working-class values can coexist with capitalist values within a predominantly capitalist context. Anticipating the positions of Lebowitz and Wright, Thompson said, "It is false to assume that because the economy of the country is predominantly capitalist, then every other aspect of our society must be organised in the interests of the capitalist system . . . there are aspects of modern society which are in origin and operation profoundly anti-capitalist."[27] For her, the welfare state opposed capitalism and reflected the long fight for it by generations of socialists.[28]

The class struggle analysis of the welfare state was also taken up by welfare and social work theorists Paul Corrigan and Peter Leonard. With reference to the British case, Corrigan tells us that "the major political force to be understood in terms of welfare provision is the working class. At all stages the working class struggle has had some form of effect upon the provision of welfare in the UK."[29] Furthermore, Leonard stated, "The role of class struggle is also crucial to our understanding of the development of the welfare state. In Britain, the Labour Party and the trade union movement have been vital to the growth of education, health and social services."[30] Both authors were clear that capitalism had needs that the state welfare was suited to meet, but the influence of the working class was certainly not to be underestimated. They recognized that to understand the emergence of the welfare state any accurate attempt to do so must situate the analysis within the context of class struggle.

Acknowledging the importance of class struggle was also accepted by welfare theorist Norman Ginsburg. Class conflict, he said, was instrumental, with both capital and labor influential.

Recognizing the welfare state under capitalism as ultimately an institution of the capitalist state, Ginsburg, like Saville, first contends that welfare has functional advantages for capitalism in that it is primarily concerned with the maintenance and reproduction of capitalist social relations.[31] This, however, does not preclude labor from influencing welfare. Although rightly arguing that the welfare state should not be considered as the unimpeded success of labor, as a class labor has nevertheless been influential. "Specific reforms have come about as the result of pressure from the organised working class . . . and the threat of the unorganised working class."[32] Thus, alongside what Ginsburg terms as enlightened members of the bourgeoisie recognizing what is required to secure the conditions of capitalism's reproduction, labor can also be identified as having determined the nature of welfare provision. Ginsburg ascribes greater authority to capital; however, the class struggle as a whole is significant: "The welfare state has been formed around the contradiction and conflicts of capitalist development in specific historical contexts."[33]

In their analysis of the potential the welfare labor force has to initiate radical change, social work scholars Steve Bolger, Paul Corrigan, Jan Docking, and Nick Frost recognize the dialectical nature of the welfare state. The capitalist state, they say, is constituted by class struggle, with both labor and capital historically determining its operation and organization. It does not operate directly under the influence of capital. That is, the state is an arena of class struggle, as are social welfare provisions. For them, capital has historically recognized the value of welfare reform, especially for the reproduction of the labor force. Additionally, labor has seized upon many of the same reforms accepted by capital, as well as agitating for further reforms, by recognizing the benefits offered to them. In this sense, these authors view the welfare state "as directly constructed by the nature of the class struggle."[34] Welfare provision cannot simply be constituted as the iron fist in a velvet glove. Instead, welfare reforms have been struggled for by labor, as well as accepted, at various points and to varying degrees, by capital. Therefore, "welfare interventions *of one form or another* became central to both the capitalist class and the working class."[35]

Welfare State Reforms and the Class Struggle

Labor can and has influenced the development of welfare under capitalism. As a result it is important to examine the extent to which the state can be utilized by labor to further its interests, and the degree to which welfare measures can be considered anti-capitalist. The role and nature of state welfare reforms has been subject to significant debate among Marxists.

Often dominating Marxism has been a criticism of state reforms. Rather than an overt criticism of the specific intentions of each individual reform, such as legislation that may expand social security entitlements, enhance state healthcare provisions, or increase welfare expenditures, etc., the primary Marxist criticism has been directed to the overall intention of reforms. Marxist theory understands that state reforms have the primary purpose of appeasing the working class, placating their anger, to secure the long-term survival of capitalism. Reforms that may benefit labor and initially appear to be in opposition to the needs and values of capitalism, are argued as having the long-term intention of ensuring the continued acceptance of capitalism among the working-class. And, subsequently, the continuation and maintenance of capitalist social relations. As Ralph Miliband posited, "In order to control the actions of labor and ensure their maintenance as effective producers, the state must often act, introducing policies and reforms that the state might not normally consider."[36]

Implemented by the state under the guidance of bourgeois governments, and often supported by some, though not always all elements of capital, social reforms are invoked to ensure capitalism's long-term stability. Consequently, such reforms, Miliband proclaims, "do not form part of a coherent and comprehensive strategy of change."[37] Advocates of social reforms, he asserts, have not been concerned with the advancement of socialism.

Reformism as Strategy

Though Miliband, among other Marxists, was adamant that social reforms should not be understood to support the gradual transformation of capitalism, this is not to say that reforms are not important. Indeed, they are vital as part of the class struggle. For Erik Olin Wright, reforms introduced by the state under capitalism have the potential to be anti-capitalist if they are underpinned by egalitarian, democratic, and solidaristic values. Consequently, they can "make the system as a whole function in a less purely capitalistic way."[38] Rather than dismissing the potential of reforms altogether, the intentions of reforms must be understood. Miliband distinguishes between social reforms, associated with those who wish to regulate and tame capitalism but not abolish it, and then reformism as a tactical philosophy that is part of the Marxist tradition. When considering the issue of reforms, it is not that in themselves they are inherently negative or have no real value for labor; it is their use and purpose that must be considered in terms of whether they can be understood to advance the class struggle and oppose exploitation and oppression.

While the advancement of reforms as an end in themselves has been criticized within Marxist theory, reforms have nonetheless commonly been identified as integral to a wider revolutionary strategy to abolish capitalism, having been, according to Miliband, "an intrinsic part of the Marxist tradition."[39] Reformism as a tactical philosophy involves the pursuance, within the context of capitalism, of varying legislative and policy reforms, including welfare. Yet, while feasibly fighting for the same reforms as individuals whose political and economic intentions are only to modify capitalism, Marxists of this persuasion "do not consider such reforms as being their ultimate purpose." Miliband points out that "these are at best steps and partial means towards a much larger purpose, which is declared to be the 'overthrow' of capitalism."[40] For Marxists, the tactical benefits of reforms is that they "chip away at the structures of capitalism."[41]

Marx and Engels

Reformism as a tactical tradition has its origins in the proclamations of Marx and Engels. Chapter 3 will illustrate this more succinctly with an examination of their position in relation to factory legislation and the regulation of the working day in Britain during the nineteenth century. For now, their attitude can be exemplified by Marx in his *Address of the Central Committee to the Communist League* in 1850.

Reflecting upon events in Germany at the time, where capital was rapidly solidifying its influence over the state, outmaneuvering the representatives of feudalism, Marx cautiously welcomed the transformation from feudalism to bourgeoise democracy. But he categorically asserted that labor should in no way form a coalition with capital. Instead, labor should ensure that it has its own independent organization from which it could influence the progression of the revolution beyond that from which capital would rest and claim victory, ensuring that the revolution was permanent until capitalism was abolished. Preempting criticisms of social reformers, Marx identifies the dangers of social reforms offered to labor by capital to quell any further discontent, arguing that the policies of state employment and welfare measures promoted by capital had the purpose "to bribe the workers with a more or less disguised form of alms and to break their revolutionary strength by temporarily rendering their situation tolerable."[42]

For Marx, it was inevitable that capital, once directly and indirectly in a position of power, would offer concessions to avert labor from agitating for further revolutionary developments. Yet he does not dismiss such reforms. In what arguably came to characterize the classical Marxist position in relation to reforms, Marx argues that labor should both accept the reforms offered and utilize them to further the revolution, constantly attempting to modify and expand them until they can be utilized for attacking the class structure of capitalism. Labor "must drive the proposals of the democrats to their logical extreme . . . and transform these proposals into direct attacks on private property. If, for instance, the bourgeoisie propose the purchase of the railways and factories, the workers must demand that these railways and factories simply be confiscated by the state without compensation."[43] For Marx, reforms were part of a wider revolutionary strategy. Progressive policies proposed by capital should, if meaningful, be embraced until they reflected and served the interests of labor. Not only was he asserting the advantages of reforms for revolutionary transformation, but he was arguing that reforms had the potential, if influenced sufficiently by labor, to reflect the values of the working class while operating within a wider capitalist context.

Rosa Luxemburg, Karl Kautsky, and V. I. Lenin

Similar positions to Marx's were adopted by some of the most notable Marxists of the classical tradition. Rosa Luxemburg vehemently opposed the pursuance of social reforms and the notion that capitalism could be gradually transformed to a more socialistic orientation and character, as epitomized by her berating of Eduard Bernstein's revisionist position. Nonetheless she recognized that reforms had a prominent role within the eventual abolition of capitalism as part of a revolutionary agenda. In *Reform and Revolution*, Luxemburg was clear in her support for reforms, arguing that in one sense her position, and that of the German SDP, was no different to the revisionist position of Bernstein, in that both supported reforms for the "immediate amelioration of the workers' condition—an objective common to our party program as well as revisionism."[44] For Luxemburg, the pursuance of reforms through democratic and parliamentary methods, as well as offering instant benefits to labor, were intended, along with industrial action, as part of a wider method of raising working-class consciousness: "Trade union and parliamentary practice are vastly important in so far as they make socialistic the *awareness*, the consciousness, of the proletariat and help organize it as a class."[45]

A contemporary of Luxemburg, Karl Kautsky, in *The Class*

Struggle, a statement reflecting the Erfurt Program adopted by the German SDP in 1891, also accepted the importance of reforms. Prior to the start of the twentieth century, Kautsky exemplified orthodox Marxism. For him, reforms, proposed by capital, were frequently utilized as a method of social control and a means of protecting capitalist property relations: "The possessing classes have been trying to prevent the threatened downfall of the system of private property . . . that is to say, to prevent revolution. Social reform is the name they give to their perpetual tinkerings . . . for the sake of removing this or that effect of private property."[46] Yet Kautsky clearly asserted that there existed advantages to social reforms for labor. For him, the downfall of capitalism was inescapable because capitalism's evolution would thrust more and more individuals into poverty and oppression, resulting in a compulsion to oppose the existence of private property. However, the transformation to socialism could be accelerated by the actions of labor. The working class, Kautsky asserted, should exhibit extreme caution with regard to the social reforms offered by capital, but this should not stifle their efforts to advance their conditions within the context of capitalism. Reforms were both useful for labor and the advancement to socialism: "Reforms may be supported from the revolutionary standpoint . . . they hasten the course of events."[47]

Lenin, despite his reputation for pursuing insurrectionary methods, recognized the power of reforms introduced within the context of capitalism for the immediate benefit of labor and facilitating capitalism's abolition. He welcomed reforms as essential for any revolutionary agenda. As Miliband wrote, Lenin's "whole work is permeated by firm approval for the struggle for partial reforms of every sort, including the most modest 'economic' reforms."[48] Prior to the turn of the twentieth century, in the *Draft and Explanation of a Programme for the Social-Democratic Party*, Lenin made clear his approval of the pursuance of immediate reforms, ranging from universal adult suffrage, an eight-hour day, to ensuring that employers were legally responsible for injuries incurred by the labor force and providing medical support. Arguing approvingly,

Lenin proclaimed, "The fight for concessions, for improved living conditions, wages and working hours . . . means that the Russian workers are making tremendous progress, and that is why the attention of the Social-Democratic Party and all class-conscious workers should be concentrated mainly on this struggle."[49]

Although Lenin initially renounced direct involvement in parliamentary activities, his repudiation was revoked on his own accord. He recognized, as Paul Le Blanc makes clear, that engagement with legislative institutions would not only support labor's agitation for legal reforms but would enhance their ability to influence wider struggles for reforms.[50] As Lenin stated in 1913, "The Marxists, far from lagging behind, are definitely in the lead in making practical use of reforms, and in fighting for them."[51] Whereas the October Revolution of 1917 exemplified insurrectionary methods, that does not mean Lenin abandoned the importance of reforms for further revolutions in the years following. As he made clear in *"Left-Wing" Communism: An Infantile Disorder*, he was critical of revolutionary agendas that focused only on illegal methods and refused to fight for reforms: "Revolutionaries who are incapable of combining illegal forms of struggle with *every* form of legal struggle are poor revolutionaries indeed."[52]

Austro-Marxism

Accepting reforms as part of a revolutionary agenda and positioning welfare at the heart of this permeated the Austro-Marxist tradition. Epitomized by figures such as Otto Bauer, Karl Renner, and Rudolf Hilferding, leading members of the Austrian Social Democratic Party (SDAP) during the first three decades of the twentieth century, Austro-Marxism, while adhering to many principles of Marxism, such as the class struggle, historical materialism, and the abolition of capitalism, embraced a system of parliamentary reform for the establishment of socialism. Insurrectionary tactics, though by no means eschewed, were to be employed only if needed to defend working-class gains.[53] For Bauer, parliamentary activities had the initial advantage of raising the political consciousness of labor. Moreover, it offered workers the opportunity to fight for policies reflecting their values. As Bauer argued, "Parliament is the indispensable tool of the great movement of the working class: a means for the education of the worker masses, an instrument through which the working class at least from time to time can implement one of its demands."[54]

As with Marx and Engels before them, the Austro-Marxists were aware of the potential for social reforms to be utilized by capital for social control. Yet throughout much of the late nineteenth and early twentieth centuries Austro-Marxism made explicit the value of fighting for welfare reforms to advance the abolition of capitalism. Achieved through legal means, it was essential that the working class seize control of the state to ensure socialism, which required the labor movement to embrace the democratic process. Acting as the vanguard, the SDAP would reflect the values of the working class, pursuing a parliamentary majority to encourage and force through reforms that would accelerate socialism's victory.

No clearer statement was presented about the fundamental role of reforms, including welfare, for Austro-Marxism, than by Bauer in the *Programme of the Social Democratic Workers Party of German Austria* in 1926, more commonly referred to as the Linz program. Here, Bauer was adamant that the purpose of the SDAP was to win control of the state and "place it in the service of the working class, to adapt the state apparatus to its needs," relieving capital of its wealth and ownership of the means of production in exchange for common ownership. As part of this agenda, the SDAP identified as essential the expansion of unemployment assistance in the form of public works, financial benefits and education programs, municipal housing, greater generosity for those disabled, old age and sickness support, and the provision of childcare, healthcare, and maternity support, among other measures. For Bauer and the SDAP, such reforms were necessary for the immediate alleviation of labor's conditions, and, more principally, for their reflection of working-class values and that they were essential for the transition to socialism.[55] Reforms, as Ewa Czerwinska-Schupp asserts, were conceptualized by the Austro-Marxists as having the potential to eradicate capitalism's social and economic foundations.[56] This spirit was embodied in the actions of the municipal government of Vienna during the 1920s, led by the SDAP, with the expansion of municipal welfare and public services, most notably housing, health, and education, giving rise to its moniker of "Red Vienna."[57]

Reforms and Labor

Reforms, although correctly identified as potential barriers to the advancement of socialism when implemented by capital, nevertheless occupy a seminal role within Marxist theory, where they have been considered integral to combating exploitation and oppression. However, a glaring truth must be acknowledged. Reforms, including welfare, when advocated by certain sections of the labor movement, have not always been enacted as part of wider efforts to overturn capitalism. Reforms have been proposed by various quarters of the labor movement solely to mitigate and alleviate the existing conditions of labor under capitalism, and not capitalism's abolition.

Reforms have been integral to the agendas of social reformist social democratic parties and labor unions. But, despite only seeking to reform capitalism, social democratic parties have been "major agencies for the advancement of demands from below . . . [and] have served to articulate grievances and mobilize discontent."[58] During the course of the twentieth century, social democratic governments were central to the progress experienced by the labor movement, which benefited greatly in terms of daily living conditions from the enactment of social reforms, such as welfare, especially during the postwar era, particularly in Europe. In conjunction with the actions of organized labor and wider pressure from below, Miliband points out that although social democratic parties have historically acted as a bulwark against the more radical ambitions of the left wing of the labor movement, the coalition between social democratic parties and organized labor has nonetheless been instrumental in advancing working-class conditions.

Objections can certainly be made regarding the ambitions of social democratic parties, and their historical record for failing to "press ahead with reforms capable of advancing the 'structural' transformation of the social order."[59] As such, it is without doubt the case that within the advanced capitalist nations, reforms, including welfare, have not eradicated oppression and exploitation. But they have, even if their intention has not been to assist in the transformation of capitalism to socialism, contributed greatly to combating oppression and exploitation. Asserting this, Miliband says, "They have, at different levels for different parts of the working class, served to improve the conditions in which domination and exploitation are experienced."[60] Furthermore, reiterating the position of Erik Olin Wright, while social democratic reforms may not have been implemented to encourage capitalism's eradication, their decommodification meant they have the potential to be utilized for anti-capitalist purposes.

In this sense, reforms implemented in this context have also significantly contributed to the class struggle, advancing the interests of labor, helping workers to oppose exploitation, oppression, and degradation. Although recognizing many of the limits of, and disadvantages to, social democratic parties and labor organizations, labor writer Michael Yates correctly asserts that struggles by labor, and their political representatives, for reforms within the context of capitalism "have resulted in tremendous and positive changes in the lives of the oppressed and expropriated."[61] As the actions of the classical Marxists illustrated, such reforms should not be disregarded, even if they originated from a political context of social reformism; instead they should be embraced and utilized as part of the class struggle. Lenin proclaimed in 1913 that "the Marxists recognise struggle for reforms, i.e., for measures that improve the conditions of the working people without destroying the power of the ruling class."[62] The qualitative nature of many reforms created and implemented under capitalism have the potential to offer a base from which to obstruct capital, and act as a means of opposing oppression and exploitation, and are thus significant for labor within the class struggle.

—— 3 ——

Marx and Engels on Social Policy

P revious Marxist analyses of welfare remain indispensable
to any understanding of social policy, providing an invaluable theoretical source. But Marxism is a rich tapestry of
interpretations and includes the works of Marx and Engels as well
as those inspired by them who, utilizing Marxist concepts, have
adopted "Marxian" perspectives. Arguably, those who have contributed most to a Marxist understanding of welfare have drawn
less from the direct writings of Marx and Engels and more from
the rich intellectual heritage they inspired. And though providing
valuable insights, this has resulted in a tendency to underappre-
ciate the relevance of Marx and Engels to make sense of social
policy, and subsequent welfare provision.

A partial explanation for the lack of direct reference to Marx
and Engels is the perceived understanding that they had little to
say about welfare. Given the embryonic nature of welfare for much
of the nineteenth century, it is indeed the case that only occasional
reference to comparable phenomena exists within their social
theory. However, a close inspection of the work of both theorists
reveals a wealth of astute observations and analyses of historical and political developments that provide significant clues as

to how they may have approached the subject. Their analysis of factory legislation provides an invaluable source of information from which it is possible to piece together how they may have conceived the subject in a more theoretical form. Embedded within their writings on phenomena comparable to social policy the clear foundations for a Marxist understanding of welfare policy grounded within the context of the class struggle can be found.

Factory Legislation and the 10 Hours' Bill

In his opening address to the First International in 1864, acknowledging that the British labor movement had experienced a stagnation of its revolutionary fortunes for more than a decade, Marx was clear there had not been a complete absence of success. Of significance was the enactment of the 10 Hours' Bill in 1847, achieved, Marx admirably argued, after thirty years of exhaustive class struggle. Strenuously endorsing its implementation, Marx emphatically defined it as a victory for the working-class.[1] Barring public health legislation, direct state intervention in British society for social purposes was in its infancy during this era. Nonetheless, the growth of factory legislation was something he examined in detail. Concerned primarily with regulating the length of the working day and the conditions of the reproduction of labor, Marx was unambiguous in recognizing the 10 Hours' Bill as positive for labor. "The immense physical, moral and intellectual benefits hence accruing to the factory operatives," Marx contended "are now acknowledged on all sides."[2]

The 10 Hours' Bill had its origins in the first stage of Britain's industrial supremacy. The catalyst for the country's economic growth during the first half of the nineteenth century was the expansion of the textile trade, in particular cotton, described by Eric Hobsbawm as "the pacemaker of industrial change."[3] Stimulating the growth of an industrial system, carved from this economic revolution was, as E. P. Thompson reminds us, the working class.[4] Although far from a homogeneous group, a collective class consciousness nonetheless developed in opposition to that of capital, allowing for the growth of what Thompson described as "a working-class structure of feeling."[5] That a working-class consciousness was sweeping through the labor force, Hobsbawm contended, was evidenced by the great upsurge of agitation in the first four decades of the nineteenth century. At the heart of labor's discontent was a growing awareness of its exploitation as their status evolved to one of subservience to the authority of capital. Upon this grew an acute awareness of injustice and deep concern for independence and security. Thompson found that "the early years of the 1830s" were "aflame with agitations which turned on issues in which wages were of secondary importance."[6] One such grievance was regulating the length of the working day.

For Marx, there existed definite circumstances that acted to place a ceiling on the maximum duration of the working day.[7] First, there were the physical limitations of workers, with all members of the labor force having a finite quantity of energy that could be expended before the need to eat, sleep, and rest was required. Second was ensuring that labor had its intellectual and social needs fulfilled. These physical and mental limitations, however, Marx stressed, came into conflict with the imperatives of capital. Capitalism is defined by its insatiable appetite for the amassing of greater quantities of surplus value to feed its need for continuing expansion. As Marx exuberantly declared, "Accumulate, accumulate! That is Moses and the prophets."[8] Describing this as capital's "single life impulse," Marx asserted that, from the perspective of the individual capitalist, the length of the working day would ideally be twenty-four hours.[9] Every conceivable moment was an opportunity to generate surplus value, with any disposable time labor may have to itself denying capitalism of further fortune.[10]

Recognizing that capital, given the opportunity, would utilize as much of the working day as possible for surplus value production, Marx was reflecting upon the significance of absolute surplus value, which is predicated upon the length of the working day. As a means of accumulation, prolongation of the working day accrues advantages depending upon the division between time required for socially necessary labor, on the one hand, and surplus labor on the other, with greater time for surplus labor determining the effectiveness of any protraction of the working day. Accumulation grounded upon the formation of absolute surplus value reigned as a preeminent means of exploitation for much of the first half of the nineteenth century. As Hobsbawm reasoned, as late as the 1840s there remained "plenty of hard-headed men who took the view that the only way to make profits was to pay the lowest money-wages for the longest hours."[11]

Driven by the desire for ever greater wealth, overexploitation of labor power was fundamental to the system, and, observing the zealous pursuit of this, Marx was alive to capital's violation of the limits to the working day: "In its blind unrestrainable passion capital oversteps not only the moral, but even the merely physical maximum bounds of the working-day."[12] As a consequence, "It usurps the time for growth, development, and healthy maintenance of the body."[13] In response, labor retaliated, demanding a 'normal' working day, allowing workers the time to replenish labor power. For this reason, Marx unequivocally argued that the length of the working day was a matter of class conflict: "The determination of what is a working-day, presents itself as the result of a struggle . . . between collective capital . . . and collective labour."[14]

Class Struggle and the Working Day

Working-class agitation reached palpable heights between 1830 and the mid-1840s. Prior to 1833 all previous factory legislation had been feebly enforced.[15] Only with the Factory Act of that year did any reason exist to take it seriously. The legislation of 1833 primarily regulated the working practices of children.[16] Yet, despite its limited reach, it aroused fierce acrimony among the bourgeoisie. But, implemented in an era of mounting working-class strength, it was followed in 1844 with additional legislation in which women over eighteen were the centerpiece, limiting them to twelve hours a day. Even then, Parliament continued to resist the full implementation of a ten-hour day.[17] Nevertheless, in 1847, as the authority of the working class in Britain peaked under the influence of Chartism, the 10 Hours' Bill was introduced. Writing three years after its passing, Engels was clear: "The Ten Hours' Bill was carried after a long and violent struggle, which had gone on for forty years in Parliament . . . and in every factory and workshop in the manufacturing districts."[18]

From its inception, capital attempted to sabotage the legislation, clinging to intensive exploitation methods of long hours and low pay. And as the fortunes of the working class declined after 1848, capital's opposition intensified.[19] For the following two years, efforts were made by capital to elude the law. This culminated in 1850 with the 10 Hours' Bill declared ineffective, as manufacturers introduced a relay system whereby women and children, although not working more than the legal requirement, worked shifts spread out during the day, which extended the absolute length of the working day to fifteen hours.[20]

In these circumstances labor rebelled. Drawing upon the testimonies of Factory Inspectors, Marx illustrates this with the response of one who "urgently warned the Government that the antagonism of classes had arrived at an incredible tension."[21] In response, the Factory Act of 1850 was passed which, while legislating the length of time women and young people worked to ten and a half hours, could only be enacted within a twelve-hour period, preventing any opportunity to continue the relay system. By 1853, with the legislation extended to limit the working hours of children, given the centrality of women, young people, and children to manufacturing operations, the act indirectly regulated the working day of all workers in industries covered by the legislation, including adult males.[22] From here on, as Marx noted, increasingly more industries came under the regulation of the law: "After the factory magnates had resigned themselves and become reconciled to the inevitable, the power of resistance of capital gradually weakened, whilst at the same time the power of attack of the working class grew."[23]

Although epitomizing the struggle, the 10 Hours' Bill of 1847 did not represent the initial advance by labor, nor did it reflect the final word on the issue. Indeed, it was a period of three decades within which labor primarily fought for legislation, with this period characterized, as Paul Sweezy describes it, as "a series of sharp political struggles," a consequence of which "the workers were able to wring one concession after another from their opponents . . . until by 1860 the principle of limitation of the working day was so firmly established that it could no longer be challenged."[24] The magnitude of these reforms, Marx asserted, was immense; they represented "the victory of a principle; it was the first time . . . the political economy of the middle class succumbed to the political economy of the working class."[25]

For Marx, the 10 Hours' Bill was a triumph of working-class values over those of capital, and it showed that such values could exist within the context of capitalism. The seeds of socialism, therefore, could conceivably be sowed under capitalism through radical reform. Furthermore, Marx clearly indicated that the state could be used as an instrument to act in the interests of the working class, with the state's official formulation of factory legislation "the result of a long struggle of classes."[26] With regard to this last point, although fiercely adhering to the conceptualization of the state as having the fundamental purpose of protecting capitalist property relations, Marx understood the state as more complex. As opposed to being simply an instrument of capital, Marx viewed the state as possessing a degree of freedom from capital, which, in turn, provided an opportunity for labor to influence the state to varying degrees. For Miliband, this was significant for the passing of the 10 Hours' Bill.[27] The degree of flexibility possessed by the state allowed it to react to the pressure from labor, with labor, in its struggle against capital, influencing the state to act in its interests, implementing legislation that broadly reflected its values.

If we accept that the 10 Hours' Bill is comparable to social policy within the era of advanced capitalism, its history affords an opportunity to recognize the role of class conflict as a decisive factor in the determination of social policy, and, specifically, how labor could influence the implementation and character of state welfare. Subsequently, under capitalism legislation can be determined by, and is an object of the class struggle, actively and consciously fought for by the working-class, which has the potential to determine its nature, even as it is opposed by capital. Moreover, there exists the opportunity for it to reflect to varying degrees the demands and values of labor, with Marx clearly accepting the 10 Hours' Bill as a piece of working-class legislation.

Acceptance and Self-Destruction

In the same chapter of *Capital* where Marx endorses the idea of the 10 Hours' Bill as built upon the terrain of class conflict, it is clear that despite initial reservations, the legislation was eventually accepted by capital. In this, Marx exhibits the distinctly contradictory nature of factory legislation, which could be applied much later to social policy.

Initially, as the latter half of the nineteenth century began, when capital adopted new production methods, objections by capitalists to the 10 Hours' Bill softened. One reason for this is that capital was able to grow by replacing absolute with relative surplus value production. Socially necessary labor time could be reduced by increasing the productiveness of labor through the use of advanced means of production, that is, machinery, which had the potential to reduce costs as wage-goods were made cheaper.[28] Relative surplus value production, Hobsbawm declared, came to increasingly characterize capitalist production after the 1840s when employers began to "abandon 'extensive' methods of exploitation such as lengthening hours and shortening wages for 'intensive' ones, which meant the opposite."[29] Additionally, for capital, reducing the working day was made more agreeable when the authority of labor waned. Accepting reforms was in large part because capital "no longer regarded the British working class as revolutionary."[30]

Aside from an evolution of production and the diminishing

assertiveness of labor, capital's recognition of the need to reduce the working day also significantly hinged upon acknowledging the need to offer some protection against capitalism's own destructive tendencies. Throughout his analysis, Marx refers to the invaluable need for endogenous methods of regulating capitalism. The rapacious desire by capital to accumulate ever greater quantities of surplus value moved Marx to the point of proclaiming that capital was ultimately reckless in its lack of concern for labor's lives.[31] While the experience of this led to the revolt of the working class who were subject to the physical and mental consequences of capital's recklessness and disregard for its hired "hands," the severity of exploitation, and its subsequent human costs, meant factory legislation was logical from the perspective of capital in the long term, as it was essential for the reproduction of labor.[32]

Exploitation, Marx accepted, was largely a consequence of systematic forces rooted within the structure of capitalism, specifically that of competition. "Free competition," Marx stated, "brings out the inherent laws of capitalist production, in the shape of external coercive laws having power over every individual capitalist."[33] The law of competition, Marx argued, was gradually becoming accepted by some within the bourgeoisie as a threat to the long-term viability of capitalism, given the compulsion of over-exploitation that emerged from it. Voluntary regulation was not an option due to the risk of some individual capitalists opting not to regulate, resulting in them gaining a competitive advantage over those who did. Therefore, to avoid excessive exploitation within the system, mandatory regulation was accepted if there was to be long-term protection of the source of surplus value.[34] This compulsion, Marx decreed, was derived externally in the form of the state, with capital acknowledging the necessity of state intervention.[35] That the state, Sweezy asserted, would act in such a way should be no surprise, with the solution to overexploitation requiring state intervention to secure long-term economic stability.[36]

For Marx, as well as for some within the bourgeoisie—increasingly the case by the late 1860s—the necessity of regulating the working day was its potential to regulate capitalism's own instinctive desire for expanded production. The intense exploitation of labor had the potential to annihilate the basis of surplus value, with the possibility that capitalism would become the victim of its own deep-seated destructive tendencies. Capital had to accept the regulation of the working day as the only cogent choice to ensure its own survival. Making an analogy with capitalism's ecological exploitation, Marx argued: "Apart from the working-class movement that daily grew more threatening, the limiting of factory labour was dictated by the same necessity which spread guano over the English fields. The same blind eagerness for plunder that in one case exhausted the soil, had, in the other, torn up by the roots the living force of the nation."[37]

The Containment of Contradictions

Although brief, the above quote from Marx is significant, as it attempts to unite the two strands of thought he exhibited in relation to social legislation. He reiterates the vital role labor played in influencing the development of factory legislation. But Marx acknowledges that the assistance it offered to labor was also advantageous for capital. Capitalism's destructive inclination to overexploit labor power mirrored capital's tendency to overexploit nature. The imperialist ventures waged by Britain in the nineteenth century to amass large quantities of guano from as far away as the South Atlantic, to spread on the fields of Britain to replenish the nutrients of the soil, was also reflected in the imposition of state regulation to prevent the overexploitation of labor power. Under capitalism, labor can successfully fight for reforms and influence the state to enact policies that can legitimately be conceived as working class in character, but which also have the advantage of supporting capitalism by regulating the exploitative character of capital in the short term for the long-term survival of conditions that are conducive to surplus value creation.

Unequivocally, for Marx, a central prerequisite of capitalism was its effort to continually expand through amassing greater quantities of surplus value with each business cycle. Nonetheless, this innate compulsion for expansion and voracious appetite for surplus value are capitalism's most destructive defects. Like Freud's death drive, which has the goal of propelling the individual to self-annihilation, capitalism, in its preoccupation to satisfy its inherent need for accumulation on an ever-greater scale, has its own *Thanatos*. As the source of profit, the gradual depletion of working-class energy would soon starve capitalism of its oxygen. As the death drive requires suppression if humanity is to continue, so capitalism's own seeds of destruction must be repressed. Although factory legislation could never eradicate the impulse, Marx recognized that it had the purpose of regulating capitalism's unbridled inclination for overexploitation. By limiting the length of time labor could be exploited, for Marx legislation was tasked with the function of preserving and protecting labor power for the long-term benefit of capital. Subsequently, Marx recognized that, in addition to legislation being a mechanism utilized by labor to defend itself against severe exploitation, it also served to protect labor against some of the worst physical and mental consequences of overexploitation for the benefit of capital.

Accepting the benefits of the factory acts as a method of regulating the exploitation of labor and to ensure the reproduction of labor power, Marx sowed the seeds for what would become a prominent principle within contemporary Marxist understandings of welfare. He considered that an essential need of capitalism was to maintain the productiveness of labor for the long-term security of the economy. Marx understood that capitalism required exogenous methods that would ensure the continued productiveness of labor power to secure capital's long-term interests. The centrality of the state's formulation of social legislation for this purpose was apparent to Marx as well as to an increasing number of the bourgeoisie, with Marx arguing this would not be forthcoming "unless under compulsion of society."[38] In this, the basis of many of the core assertions associated with Marxist theorists of welfare during the 1970s and early 1980s can be identified. For instance, James O'Connor stressed the vital social consumption function of the state, whereby the costs of labor's reproduction through various welfare services, specifically to reproduce labor power for capital's benefit, is primarily socialized.[39] Additionally, Ian Gough also identified the reproduction of labor power as central to the operation of the welfare state.[40]

Class Struggle and Social Policy

From his analysis of factory legislation, Marx perceived social legislation as having functional advantages for capitalism. But any accurate understanding cannot solely be achieved in terms of analyzing the advantages it has for capitalism alone. That the working class, as part of its struggles against capital, was essential to the establishment of factory legislation is not in doubt. For Marx, analyzing only the functional benefits of social legislation for capitalism risked extrapolating any understanding of it from a fundamental characteristic of capitalism. It is a system of classes in perpetual opposition to each other.

Class antagonism is inherent to capitalism. Class conflict is a determinant of both economic and social evolution.[41] It is within this context that Marx and Engels situated their analysis of social legislation; it must be understood within a wider framework, with the outcome the result of the relative strength of labor and capital. As Marx emphasized: "The creation of a normal working-day is . . . the product of a protracted civil war . . . between the capitalist class and the working class."[42]

Drawing upon Marx and Engels's understanding of factory legislation, the development of social policy and welfare must be understood as emerging from, and shaped by, class conflict. Social policy has encapsulated in its organization and operation the antagonistic social relations of capitalist society. Marx and Engels firmly viewed social legislation as shaped by the active class consciousness of both capital and labor, which also explains the evolution of social policy. Rather than perceiving social policy as primarily an instrument of capital to facilitate the expansion of surplus value and viewing it only in terms of its functional advantages for capital, social policy and welfare services must instead be understood as a platform upon which class conflict is fought.

Marx recognized the formulation of social legislation is greatly influenced by both the political judgments of capital as well as the pressures from labor.[43] Marx and Engels demonstrated that labor consciously seized upon the 10 Hours' Bill as an instrument of reform from which they gained advantage. Yet calculated decisions based upon the class interests of capital were central to the eventual enactment and implementation of factory legislation. As the ebb and flow of the class struggle swung in favor of labor prior to 1847, calculating what was in their best interests, capital was forced to gradually pass initial factory acts to stave off the enveloping tide of labor's resistance. While a modest effort in comparison to welfare measures within many contemporary monopoly capitalist societies, factory legislation was nonetheless both a means via which labor attempted to assert and defend itself, as well as an institutional method through which capital attempted to continue its dominance.

Marx, Engels, and State Reforms

Chapter 2 demonstrated that both Marx and Engels, while displaying open hesitancy of, and condemnation toward state reforms under capitalism, nonetheless accepted that reforms offered an opportunity to advance labor's demands. Accepting the 10 Hours' Bill as an early example of state social policy was recognition of the importance of such legislation to advance the position of labor and aid the transition to socialism. Agreeing with Marx's assertion that it reflected the political economy of labor, historian Dorothy Thompson described the legislation as "an essentially anti-capitalist piece of legislation."[44] Marx, Ramesh Mishra argues, did not flinch from endorsing the notion that the working class could significantly modify capitalism, forcing through change that could reform the economy from within, with social legislation being one such instrument for this, and labor having the ability to impose its own values upon the state.[45]

As part of a Marxist reformist strategy, social policies can be accepted as having the potential to reflect the values of labor and therefore be central to the transition to socialism. Yet, as Marx and Engels's analysis of the 10 Hours' Bill exemplifies, it must not be ignored that such polices can be utilized by both labor *and* capital. That the state acts to reproduce capitalist social relations is not in doubt. For Sweezy, the state is "an instrument in the hands of the ruling class for enforcing and guaranteeing the stability of the class structure itself."[46] However, labor has the capacity to influence social legislation from which it benefits, and Sweezy accepts the 10 Hours' Bill as an example. Yet he recognized limits to this. Concessions capital make are only granted if they do not threaten the principles upon which capitalism operates; even if they may be counterproductive for capital in the short term, they preserve the stability of capitalism in the longterm.[47] Moreover, despite Thompson's assertions that labor can, and has, significantly influenced the development of welfare, she too recognized that welfare reforms have also been achieved as a consequence of an alliance between labor and capital.[48] Reflecting upon the complexity of welfare and social policy under capitalism, and subsequently their dialectical nature, Ralph Miliband argues that social institutions are rarely towering instruments of capital's oppression, but neither can they be considered the preserve of labor. They can equally be utilized, and fought for, by both classes for their own benefit and assume the form of centers of class conflict, as instruments to advance the interests of both capital and labor.[49] This duality of understanding is glaringly present in Marx and Engels's conception of the 10 Hours' Bill.

Rather than conceding that social policy has been primarily initiated by capital to support the accumulation process and as a means of solidifying its hegemonic dominance, both of which have undoubtedly been a factor in its evolution, it must instead be understood as a dialectical phenomenon. As well as the influence of capital upon its organization and character, both the direct and indirect determining pressures of labor have been significant. Direct pressure means the actions of organized labor and their political representatives, including social democratic governments as well as socialist politicians. Indirect pressure pertains to the actions of the labor movement, the very existence of the working class, and the perceived potential they have for social unrest which, when acknowledged by capital and middle-class reformers, prompts reform to contain possible conflict. However, contemporary Marxist literature has often neglected this; what Saville saw as a significant determining force in the creation of social policy: "the pressures which have come from the mass of the population."[50]

That it could be argued as a contradictory position to proclaim that social policy has been influenced and shaped by both capital and labor, reflecting the values and needs of both classes, expresses the real contradictory nature of social policy and welfare services under capitalism. Operating and organized within the context of class struggle, the state, while functioning for the long-term interests of capitalism, nonetheless reflects the balance of class forces, operating in a way that reflects the interests of the capitalist class as a whole, and, to some extent, the struggles of labor, insofar as this does not threaten capital accumulation. As Engels argued about the state, it attempts to contain and manage the irreconcilable antagonisms between capital and labor—but its ability to achieve this is strictly limited by the premium always placed on profitability.[51]

Social legislation as identified by Marx and Engels, and the growth of social policy and welfare during the last century, acutely illustrates the antagonistic relationship between capital and labor. Undoubtedly, welfare under capitalism has often displayed a disciplinary character and has been meager in provision. But it is important not to neglect the very real advantages labor has obtained from welfare programs. Often it has been "un-Marxist" to acknowledge this. But this is far from accurate. As Marx's own analysis of the 10 Hours' Bill demonstrates, while capital may come to recognize the value of welfare services and appropriate them to maintain its own dominance, such developments can nonetheless still rightly be thought of as a significant benefit to labor and reflect values that are in opposition to capital. The decommodified nature of many present welfare programs, and their collective provision via the state, stand in opposition to the basic principles of capital, as Marx proclaimed with the 10 Hours' Bill. Capitalism, with very clear limits, may exist as a system that can accommodate a certain amount of decommodification, and may also benefit from such services. A Marxist understanding of social policy is to be aware of its duality.

—— 4 ——

Capital and Welfare Expansion

M arxist-inspired welfare theorists Chris Jones and Tony Novak argue that rising standards of health, housing, and education have been, in part, a response by the state to support labor's adaptation to capitalism's need for expansion.[1] Crucially, they situate this claim within a wider class struggle context, noting that there have always existed periods when the need to maintain and reproduce the productivity of labor has been a conscious and deliberate effort on the part of capital, utilizing the state for this process. In Britain, one such period was the late nineteenth and early twentieth centuries. Influential elements within the ranks of capital championed welfare measures in response to the perceived need to enhance the productivity of labor in the face of declining economic competitiveness. This laid the foundations for the British welfare state to develop during the twentieth century.

Expansion and Decline

By the latter half of the nineteenth century, Britain had been transformed from a dynamic industrial economy to a sluggish

and conservative one.[2] While the country's initial economic dominance was based primarily on textile industries, in the 1840s heavy
industry and capital goods formed the basis of economic growth.
Stimulating this new phase was the insidious but rapid spread of
capitalism globally. The demand for British goods from newly
industrialized nations acted as a significant stimulus for Britain's
economic expansion.

Requiring coal, steel, and iron for their growth, the newly industrialized countries turned to Britain to satisfy this demand. British
exports rapidly expanded between 1840 and 1860. At the same
time, the British economy was awash with surplus capital. Internal
sources of profitable investment were in short supply relative to
the funds available for them. Respite emerged with the railways,
which grew in response to the nation's growth but also because
they absorbed surplus capital. In addition, the newly industri-
alizing nations of the United States and Europe built railways,
with these partly funded by British capital and materials, again
absorbing surplus capital. The development of overseas markets
in this sense depicted a fundamental act of imperialism. As Harry
Magdoff observed, "When the practical limit of the railroad building was being reached in one country, outlets in another country
were sought."[3]

The transformation of Britain to an economy underpinned
by heavy industry contributed to the growth, both absolutely
and relatively, of labor as a social class. Within industries such
as engineering, the construction of the means of production,
and shipbuilding the numbers doubled between 1851 and 1881.
Coal miners grew exponentially, from approximately 200,000 in
1850 to 1.4 million on the eve of the First World War. As such, an
inevitable, and inextricably related, consequence of Britain's capitalist expansion was the rise of the working class. Although the
growth of the industrial labor force reflected Britain's economic
dominance, its position as the preeminent global economic force
was not to last. During the final decades of the nineteenth century, Britain's position relative to other nations, such as Germany

and the United States, declined. Transformations in the organization and operation of capitalism, which were embraced by newly industrialized nations, were largely rejected in Britain. A general stagnation thus characterized Britain's economic base as it entered a phase of maturity, with Britain's reluctance to adapt hampering its economic development.

In the fields of scientific innovation and production, Britain fell behind the United States and Germany. Additionally, economic concentration and monopolization, something that gave Britain's rivals further advantages, was resisted. Eric Hobsbawm put it this way: "However strongly the winds of change blew elsewhere, as soon as they crossed the Channel to Britain they grew sluggish."[4] As other nations adopted the same economic practices, Britain would lose her relative advantage. The opportunity and the means to adapt were available, but British capital was simply unwilling to do so.[5] Adaptation to new methods of production would be costly, difficult, and time-consuming. It was still possible to make profit utilizing old production methods. As such, Hobsbawm wrote, "The traditional methods of making profits had yet to be exhausted, and provided a cheaper and more convenient alternative to modernization—for a while."[6] Still, relative economic decline, and the consequences of the Long Depression (1873–1896), severely troubled many within the British ruling class.[7]

National Efficiency and Labor Productivity

Attention within the ranks of capital turned to the productivity of labor, where it was thought that a significant reason for Britain's decline was a result of labor's lack of productiveness. Perturbation regarding the quality of labor was exacerbated by the prolonged nature of the Second African War (the Second Boer War), between 1899 and 1902. Serious deficiencies regarding the physical condition of many of the British recruits emerged, a substantial proportion of whom were drawn from the working class. Due to such concerns, influential elements of capital sought solutions by adopting a position of social reform. What prevailed amounted to an attack on the principles of laissez-faire in its Victorian form. Acceptance that the state should become actively involved in maintaining the conditions of economic growth triumphed, with the provision of basic welfare measures.

The decline in Britain's economic stature was a consequence of a weak and ineffective labor force. It lacked the skill, and most of all, the physical competence, to compete with overseas labor in Germany, the United States, and Japan. While many representatives of capital agreed upon the urgency to rejuvenate British capitalism, the recommendations of social reformers to support the long-term interests of capitalism using the state exposed and exacerbated divisions among the capitalist class.[8] Proposals to increase the efficiency of labor were most advantageous to, and more easily afforded by, larger units of capital, with small enterprise in some cases openly hostile to the idea of greater state intervention. However, it was clear that in late Victorian Britain, the momentum was firmly behind an eclectic group of bourgeois social reformers, consisting of middle-class philanthropists and social researchers who exposed the extreme levels of poverty experienced by many within the working class: politicians representing the political philosophy of new Liberalism; supporters of Fabian socialism; those who wanted Britain's empire defended; and members of Britain's capitalist class who saw no other choice but to reform if the nation was to remain economically competitive. All coalesced, to varying degrees, around the acceptance that an element of state intervention was required to enhance labor productivity.

The competitiveness of the British economy was understood to pivot on the creation of a labor force with both the physical and mental aptitudes conducive to economic growth. Conservative politician Arthur Balfour argued the importance of creating an industrial character, claiming, "It is a most intolerable thing that we should permit the permanent deterioration of those who are fit for really good work. . . . Is it not very poor economy to scrap good machinery?"[9] Such a position was not the sole preserve of the political right. Support for enhancing the productivity of labor to strengthen British capitalism was openly endorsed by more progressive political forces. As Sidney Webb, a leading advocate of Fabian socialism during the late nineteenth and early twentieth century, stated in 1890, it was crucial that "a new industrial character" be created "not merely or even mainly for the comfort of the workers, but absolutely for the success of our industry in competition with the world."[10] For Fabians, the state was central to their philosophy, with socialism established upon state intervention, greater economic controls, and a re-moralization of the working class based upon education and discipline.[11]

Imperialist Expansion

Alongside attempts to enhance labor productivity, further efforts to support economic growth were made by ensuring Britain maintained its imperial dominance by focusing on overseas markets Britain had authority over. As Hobsbawm said of this era, Britain's exports exhibited "a steady flight from the modern resistant and competitive markets into the undeveloped."[12] With the nineteenth century ending, the reliance upon undeveloped markets came to mean Britain's empire. The demand created by Britain's imperial markets "become increasingly vital after the 1870s, when foreign competition became acute, and Britain sought to escape from it . . . by a flight into her dependencies."[13] With Britain's global competitiveness weakening, maintaining its empire was an economic imperative. Crucially, the maintenance of empire and the creation of an economically productive labor force were inextricably related. The health and fitness of the British working class was paramount as only an efficient nation would be able to maintain an expanding empire.[14]

A leading exponent of the national efficiency movement, Liberal politician Charles Masterman, asserted in 1901 that those concerned about the prosperity of the British Empire could not be indifferent to the conditions of the majority at its center.[15] Moreover, in the same year, Lord Rosebery, a former Liberal prime minister, proclaimed the British Empire required an "imperial race," vigorous, industrious, and in good health.[16] Such concerns helped to unite many social reformers in their pursuit of enhancing the physical and mental condition of the labor force. Fabian socialist Sidney Webb summed this up: "How can we build up an effective commonwealth—how even can we get an effective army—out of the stunted, anaemic, demoralised denizens of the slum tenements of our great cities?"[17]

Welfare Reforms

For many social reformers, national efficiency could not be disentangled from capitalism's unrestrained pursuit of profit and its consequences for the material conditions experienced by labor. Attention was given to small businesses whose survival was often predicated upon low wages to compete with larger enterprises. The actions of this section of the capitalist class were seen as an important determinant of the decline in national efficiency. Moreover, poverty, with its dire consequences for the physical condition of labor, was viewed as a threat to the empire. For the interests of capital, the exploitative activities of small business would have to be suppressed or mitigated.[18] Bourgeois social reformers understood that the social conditions experienced by many of the working class were a threat to capitalism. Welfare reforms initiated by the state would act to curb some of the most excessive negative consequences of capitalism. But rather than viewing this as a means of offering support to labor against capitalism, reforms were seen as necessary to strengthen productivity and thus enhance the vitality of British capitalism and the British Empire.[19]

Social reforms would guarantee a national minimum that no individual in society should fall below. All members of the labor force should be prescribed a certain basic minimum level of education, leisure, sanitation, and wages.[20] By enacting such welfare measures, Britain would have a labor force that would help maintain the empire. The centrality of social policy to enhancing labor productivity was made clear no more succinctly than by the individual commonly credited with laying the foundation for the expansion of Britain's welfare state after the Second World War, civil servant and Liberal Party member William Beveridge. During the first decade of the twentieth century, Beveridge proclaimed that "individual efficiency and production . . . must be the corner-stone of social policy."[21]

As the twentieth century dawned, the physical decline of Britain's labor force was not just the concern of middle-class social researchers, philanthropists, Liberal politicians, bourgeois socialists, and sections of the capitalist class. It became a matter of scientific scrutiny. In 1903, contributors to the *British Medical Journal* expressed their alarm that if the minimum necessities required for physical efficiency were not available to all, in particular nutrition, the physical decline of the British nation would prevail.[22] A year later, the report of the Interdepartmental Committee on Physical Deterioration, comprising civil servants and medical experts, was published. From this a notable extension of the state's activities was proposed. State interventions akin to welfare reforms included an extension of state regulations over environmental health conditions, as well as enhanced building and sanitary regulations, along with state encouragement of physical training and exercise. Additionally, state school medical inspections were proposed, along with a state-sponsored system ensuring that all children were sufficiently fed to support their educational development.[23]

Initially, the Conservative government of Arthur Balfour, between 1902 and 1905, resisted calls for increased state intervention, recoiling at the thought of raising taxes and increasing public expenditures. Pressure became too great, however, as concerns regarding the condition of children predominated in the national efficiency debate. Winning a landslide general election victory in 1906, the Liberal Party's period in government until the outbreak of the First World War was characterized by the adoption of social reforms that constitute the first recognizable state welfare measures implemented in Britain.[24] With the productivity of the labor force of paramount concern, substantial welfare provisions within the spheres of health and education were established. A significant foundation of the British welfare state was the 1906 Education (Provision of Meals) Act. This permitted municipalities the ability to provide free school meals for all elementary school children if parents were unable to contribute themselves. A year later, the Education (Administrative Provisions) Act of 1907 was passed, establishing medical inspections in state schools.

Almost half a century before Britain's National Health Service was established, focus on the health of the British labor force prevailed as an issue of concern for capital, as exemplified by the creation of national health insurance introduced in 1911. Many employers were concerned about the efficiency of their workers due to poor health, recognizing the need for intervention to ensure a healthier labor force.[25] Such concerns were also recognized in government, stimulating the enactment of the national health insurance program. This covered the basic health needs of some members of the working class, while the health of future members of the labor force was taken into consideration with the establishment of free school meals and medical inspections.

The implementation of welfare measures such as these should not be considered as the act of a caring benevolent state. Rather, it was an example of a state actively intervening to enhance Britain's ability to compete within an expanding global capitalist economy. Put simply, if Britain was to maintain global dominance, a strict adherence to laissez-faire had to be abandoned. Concerns once thought the sole preserve and responsibility of the individual were instead accepted as the responsibility of the state.

Growing Discontent

At the height of the Second World War, Conservative Member of

Parliament Quintin Hogg, the future Lord Hailsham, proclaimed in a debate concerning welfare provision, "If you do not give the people social reform they are going to give you social revolution."[26] Straight from the mouth of Britain's ruling class, the words of Hogg made explicit a line of reasoning that has dominated bourgeois understandings of state welfare for decades, namely that it has the potential to act as an effective method of controlling labor within the context of a precarious market and rising unemployment. By the 1880s, the impact of the Long Depression in Britain was keenly felt. Poverty and destitution prevailed for many as economic contraction continued, in conjunction with, and related to, a decline of older industries.[27] Come the middle of the decade, unemployment, even among some of the more affluent members of the working class, had reached 10 percent.[28]

As economic decline blighted the lives of many, the era witnessed the "(re)discovery" of poverty by the middle classes. For example, the investigations of Charles Booth and Seebohm Rowntree helped bring the infiltration of poverty and destitution among the working class to the attention of philanthropists and social reformers. These investigations were far from value-free. Reflecting the middle-class disposition of the researchers, a moral agenda permeated these inquiries. Primarily this pivoted around illustrating the existence of the "respectable" working-class, on the one hand, and the casual poor on the other, with such distinctions based largely upon skill and wages. For Booth, whose analyses were particularly influential, those occupying the top of the working-class hierarchy were highly skilled industrial workers, who received the highest wages, were more likely to be in regular employment, and had a greater predisposition to be members of trade unions and cooperative organizations. Languishing at the bottom of the labor force were, Booth noted, the casual poor. They were frequently unemployed and underemployed, having irregular work which subsequently meant they often depended upon casual labor, primarily in the docks and factories. Given their economic status, their incomes were often supplemented by charity.[29] For one Fabian commentator, the casual poor were "the great industrial residuum of all the industrial classes of the community."[30] Their position within the labor force epitomized Marx's conception of the reserve army of labor, a surplus labor population constituting a disposable resource for capital to be exploited when needed.[31]

As the economy contracted in the final decades of the nineteenth century, a significant consequence was the upsurge of unrest and agitation within the working classes, reaching its peak between the late 1880s and early 1890s.[32] Riots characterized major British cities, especially London, striking fear in the middle class. The protests largely consisted of impoverished and disaffected members of the casual poor demanding unemployment support, such as public works and protective tariffs.[33] Of additional concern for capital was the growing evidence of dissatisfaction among the skilled working-class as the impact of the depression spread, stimulating the growing popularity of socialist ideas and union organization.

With unemployment spreading throughout the labor force, there emerged, as historian Gareth Stedman Jones noted, the possibility that "the respectable working class, under the stress of prolonged unemployment, might throw in its lot with the casual poor."[34] The very existence of the casual poor was seen as having the potential to "contaminate" the skilled working-class.[35] The fear of a merger or alliance between both groups was in part because of a growing class consciousness, not just among skilled members of the working class, but also the casual poor and unskilled. For the British ruling class, should socialist ideas filter down to the casual poor, there existed a real threat to the capitalist social order. The growing fear of the working class was expressed succinctly by Winston Churchill in 1909, proclaiming the greatest danger to Britain was not the imperial and military ambitions of other European nations, but rather, "It is here, close at home, close at hand in the vast growing cities of England and Scotland."[36]

Burgeoning class consciousness among the casual poor and

unskilled was visible by the growth in unionism during the 1880s and 1890s. Unlike existing unions, the new unions organized workers across industries, to appeal to individuals based upon their class rather than occupation.[37] Described in 1892 by Engels as the organization of the mass of unskilled workers, the founders of the new unions were "socialists either consciously or by feeling," with their members "rough, neglected, looked down upon by the working-class aristocracy." Yet, Engels contended, the new unions were "taking the lead of the working-class movement generally."[38]

As Britain entered the last decade of the nineteenth century, throughout the working class there subsequently emerged an intensification of class consciousness. Wholesale disillusionment and hostility prevailed. With fear growing that this might intensify should an alliance be established between the skilled and unskilled members of the working class, capital made great efforts to implement measures that would divide and distinguish the skilled workers from the casual poor, with attention primarily directed toward abating the demands and grievances of the skilled group. As Stedman Jones contends, this largely meant ensuring that "the 'respectable' working class should be enabled to participate more actively within the political system."[39] It is within this context that the enactment of state welfare reforms at the start of the twentieth century can also be understood.

State Welfare as Social Control

Confronted with increasingly widespread agitation, by the early twentieth century the Liberal government was compelled to act. In the short term its actions had to defuse working-class anger, but in the long term measures had to be taken to ensure labor's allegiance to capitalism. Consequently, it was the need to curb the threat of the working class and secure political stability that particularly galvanized social reformers to implement welfare measures.[40] For many within the ruling class, inspiration for welfare reforms could be found in Germany, which, during the latter part of the nineteenth century, had introduced a system of state-sponsored social insurance. That the then Chancellor of the Exchequer, Lloyd George, was influenced by the German system was exhibited by his visit to Germany in 1908 that helped him develop an understanding of the system in practice. Additionally, Churchill expounded the need to "thrust a big slice of Bismarckianism over the whole underside of our industrial system."[41] Not only was the German system a source of inspiration in terms of delivery and administration, but its purpose was also of particular admiration.

Underpinning the German system were efforts to reduce the appeal of socialism among the labor force. This was recognized in Britain in the position of Harold Spender, an associate of Lloyd George, who in 1909 firmly asserted that social reformers in Britain would do well to take "a leaf from the book of Bismark, who dealt the heaviest blow against German socialism . . . by that great system of State insurance which now safeguards the German worker."[42] Welfare reforms were identified as essential to combat the insurgence of the working class and undermine the appeal of socialism. In this there are echoes of Arthur Balfour, who, despite his reluctance as prime minister less than a decade later to introduce reforms, in 1895 nonetheless claimed: "Social legislation . . . is not merely to be distinguished from Socialist legislation but it is its most direct opposite and its most effective antidote."[43]

As can be seen from all of this, the nature of such reforms was greatly influenced by the needs of capital, mainly the desire of those with commanding economic power to maintain economic and political stability. And so, in an effort to reduce the appeal of socialism, dilute the class consciousness of labor, and to cement division among the working class, welfare reforms were introduced to reflect capital's need to maintain economic and political stability.

Because the attraction of socialism was greatest among the skilled working class, welfare reforms were devised to appeal to this section of the labor force and largely exclude the casual poor. Tremendous efforts were made to secure the allegiance of skilled workers to the labor process, with welfare reforms designed to reinforce the social relations of capitalism. This, it was thought, could be accomplished with the introduction of work-related benefit schemes, reflecting the German social insurance system. The National Insurance Act of 1911, granting unemployment benefits and health insurance to those members of the working class in regular employment, through contributions provided by employees and the state, epitomized the Liberal government's welfare measures. Since the system was predicated upon sufficient levels of contributions, the unskilled, casually employed, and many women received little support.

Not only did this drive an effective wedge between the skilled and unskilled members of the working class, but it also contributed to greater acceptance of the capitalist state among the former. As Novak argued, this effective extension of citizenship was an attempt to incorporate skilled workers within the existing political and economic structures of society.[44] For Churchill, the goal was "to increase the stability of our institutions by giving the mass of industrial workers a direct interest in maintaining them . . . . With a 'stake in the country' in the form of insurances . . . workers will pay no attention to the vague promises of revolutionary socialism."[45] In this, the role of welfare reforms as crucial to maintain social stability was made abundantly clear.

The ruling class thus shook off the chains of a rigid laissez-faire and accepted the need for state-financed welfare reforms. An argument can be made that it was a fear-generated response to growing labor radicalism and militancy in the form of strikes and riots. As John Charlton contends, the very existence and growth of the working class between the 1880s and the eve of the First World War, as well as visible periods of working-class agitation becoming a dominant and visible feature of British society, was enough in itself for labor to have influenced the growth of state welfare.[46]

——— 5 ———

The Struggle for Welfare

The historical relationship between labor and welfare in Britain is complex. There are those, such as historian Henry Pelling, who emphatically argued, with regard to state welfare, that during the late nineteenth and early twentieth centuries the British working class was antagonistic to state intervention. "The extension of the power of the state . . . which is generally regarded as having laid the foundations of the welfare state, was by no means welcomed by members of the working class." This hostility was primarily a result of an entrenched opposition to the state itself, with workers' experience of it one of oppression and control.[1] State welfare was considered both intrusive and a means of regulating labor. Consequently, there was notable working-class suspicion of it.[2]

Among sections of the British labor force attention to welfare was considered a distraction from industrial conflict. Welfare diverted attention from struggles for job security and increased wages, and employer endorsement of social reforms laid bare capital's true position: welfare was a cheaper option than increasing wages.[3] For many within the skilled working class, industrial activity was subsequently privileged over welfare.[4] This would allow the working class to provide for themselves during times of need and thus retain their independence rather than relying upon a repressive state apparatus. As a founding member of the Labour Party, member of Parliament and future prime minister, Ramsay MacDonald, said in 1911, "If the employer pays proper wages . . . then we do not want charity and we do not want assistance at all."[5]

The introduction of state welfare was also considered a threat to established working-class organizations. Along with trade unions, workers had also engaged in various types of formal and informal cooperative self-help. A prominent example was the establishment of "friendly societies," whose membership were largely drawn from the skilled working class. Chris Jones and Tony Novak explained that such organizations were established out of necessity, as collective efforts to provide against the constant threat of poverty and economic insecurity. They were the main source of assistance during times of unemployment, sickness, and old age.[6]

At their peak at the turn of the twentieth century, membership in friendly societies was over five million, far greater than the total membership of trade unions.[7] For the most part, they opposed state provision of welfare.[8] Self-help was perceived as socially and morally preferable to reliance upon the state. State welfare was seen not only as corrosive of worker independence but also as a threat to the very existence of alternative forms of welfare provision. From the perspective of many friendly societies, support provided by the state was thought to potentially undermine their authority within the working class.

In the quarter-century preceding the First World War, possibly one of the clearest statements from within the labor movement of opposition to the provision of state reforms, including welfare, was adopted by the Socialist League of William Morris. Emphatically, they opposed most social reforms on the basis that it was beyond the capability of the capitalist state to offer policies that benefited the working class above that of capital. State welfare would only advance the position of labor once the working class had captured the state for itself.[9] Breaking away from the Social Democratic Federation (SDF) in 1884, Morris, along with Eleanor Marx and Ernest Bax, among others, established the Socialist League as a means of opposing parliamentary methods to promote reforms.

The Socialist League vehemently disputed the notion that the implementation of state reforms represented an attack on capitalism and were an aid in the transition to socialism. Pejoratively referring to reforms as characteristic of "state socialism," Morris saw little of value in socialists embracing the state and using Parliament to advance the needs of labor, with reforms doing no more than "tampering piecemeal with our Society."[10] Morris declared that if socialists entered Parliament, their radical agenda eventually would be diluted to mere modest reforms of capitalism. "The object of Parliamentary institutions is the preservation of society in its present form," with reforms instigated through Parliament no more than a means of revising the system in order to preserve it, "yielding what is absolutely necessary to popular demands in the assured hope of hushing those demands."[11] Reflecting upon the gradual development of municipal services during the last decade of the nineteenth century, including housing, Morris asserted there existed the danger of this "quasi-socialist machinery" being utilized to pacify the working class and dilute their socialist consciousness.[12] Reforms, at best, only dealt with symptoms, not causes. For Morris, the revolution could only be successful with socialists acting outside of Parliament, a policy of abstention, trying to stimulate revolutionary consciousness through the education of the working class.

The position of Morris and the Socialist League encapsulated a genuine socialist perspective during this period. It expressed opposition to making use of existing capitalist institutions, in particular the state and its quasi-socialist machinery, as part of the wider agenda to abolish capitalism. This was not an uncommon perspective. However, it was not the only one, as we have seen in previous chapters.

The State, Parliament, and Welfare Provision

A prominent Marxist advocate of the benefits of state reforms under capitalism was Henry Hyndman and the SDF, Britain's first Marxist party, albeit one that Marx and Engels criticized. The main reason for Engels's antipathy toward the SDF was that it was primarily under the authority of "young bourgeois intelligentsia" rather than the working class.[13] Later, Engels would also accuse them of having "managed to transform our theory into the rigid dogma of an orthodox sect."[14] Despite this animosity, Engels was clear in his support for their program of change, broadly accepting the SDFs 1883 manifesto, *Socialism Made Plain*.[15] Moreover, a decade later, when admiringly discussing the success of the German Social Democratic Party (SPD), he said that the position of the German SPD "is very nearly identical with that of the Social-Democratic Federation in England."[16]

It has been argued that the membership of the SDF was too small for it to have been influential within the wider labor movement. It is true that its membership never exceeded 4,000 during the late nineteenth century, but its newspaper, *Justice*, had a reach far greater than its membership would suggest. Irrespective of the numbers, the significance of the SDF lies with it being an openly Marxist organization for which reforms and state welfare were integral to its revolutionary agenda. In contrast to the position of the Socialist League, the SDF identified the fight for reforms under capitalism as fundamental in their revolutionary strategy, with many of its membership supporting reforms. It was possible to lay the foundations of socialism within a capitalist context, establishing institutions that would ease the transition from capitalism to socialism. As Henry Hyndman himself said, social reforms were "stepping stones to socialism."[17]

From the perspective of the SDF, a substantial proportion of the British working class lacked the ability and consciousness to instigate revolution. Only a well-educated and healthy labor force would be in any position to transform society. As such, during the

1880s, improvements in healthcare and housing, the introduction of free education, and an eight-hour work day were demanded. Not only would such reforms alleviate the worst excesses of capitalism, but in the long term they would strengthen the resolve of the labor force, equipping them both physically and mentally to transform society to socialism.[18] The manifesto of 1883, which Engels largely supported, called for a transitional program, which included policies such as an eight-hour day, construction of working-class homes, free schooling that included at least one free school meal, progressive taxation, and the public ownership of land and the railways.[19]

Hyndman was critical of those socialists who refused to contemplate utilizing existing institutions and democratic machinery to advance the foundations of socialism, asserting they exhibited "anarchical absurdities" and "honestly believe that all political action is harmful."[20] However, Hyndman and the SDF could not be considered "state socialists" in the sense that Morris utilized the term. For Hyndman, tactically it was clear: "Obviously, we have to work in the world as we find it and, although we must retain our definite class war principles and organization, it is as ridiculous to say that we must never co-operate with people who partly agree with us."[21] But this tactic, including forcing the capitalist state to implement policies that would help lay the foundations of socialism, was only characteristic of a transition phase between capitalism and socialism. Hyndman contended that few socialists could accept state reforms as anything more than temporary measures to alleviate working-class conditions. "The State is used for this purpose, not because we admire or even tolerate the State, but because, with all its innumerable drawbacks, it is the only machinery available for such partial improvement. We have no illusions whatever in the matter." Utilizing the state like this was done with "the deliberate intention of putting an end to the State."[22]

While there were undoubtedly sections of the labor movement opposed to reform, it was nonetheless the position of the SDF that corresponded with the Second International, a loose federation of political parties and labor organizations that was able to unite the international labor movement under the colors of Marxism, with the overthrow of capitalism its objective.[23] It strongly encouraged the working class to fight to take power. Yet it openly supported state reforms of a welfare nature for the immediate benefit of the working class, as well as aiding the broader objective of the transition to socialism.

During the period of its existence, between 1889 and 1916, the Second International supported such resolutions as an eight-hour day, which would allow time for labor to engage in political and union activity. Other resolutions supported welfare reforms for sickness, healthcare, and unemployment. The importance of utilizing Parliament was acknowledged by the Second International for "the realization of reforms of immediate interest." As a result, "We recommend to the workers of all countries to conquer political rights, and to make use of them in all legislative and administrative bodies, for the purpose of realizing the demands of the proletariat, and to gain possession of political power."[24]

Reforms and the Labor Movement

From the 1890s, the provision of state healthcare and pensions, free education until university, and the subsidization of working-class housing, were regularly debated during the annual conference of the Trades Union Congress (TUC), with majority support commonplace for such initiatives.[25] One reason for this increasing focus on reforms was the expansion of unionism to include those who were not craft workers. By the start of the twentieth century, the organized labor movement was rapidly becoming more diverse, with greater representation of unskilled members of the working class.

Unions representing craft occupations commonly offered members their own social protection, with qualification predicated upon regular contributions. Although a broad consensus existed among unions of both skilled and unskilled workers for the need to increase public expenditure for housing and education, reservations existed, primarily among craft workers with respect to state provision of social insurance.[26] This reflected the financial divisions within the working class and the advantages for its skilled members, many of whom were able to obtain social security–type benefits for themselves through union and friendly society schemes. Unions representing the less skilled, however, were not able to offer welfare support. For those earning lower wages, many of whom lived in poverty, state support in times of unemployment and sickness resonated, given that neither they nor their unions could secure such help.[27] For this section of the working class, state welfare represented a potentially vital means of support against their exploitation.

By the turn of the century, the Labour Party recognized the state as integral to class struggle and supported state welfare as instrumental to combating exploitation. For the leaders of the Labour Party, the state was understood to reflect the community and wider society rather than simply operating as an instrument of class rule. As historian Stuart Macintyre asserted, Labour representatives perceived state ownership and state social reforms as the means through which wealth and power would be much more evenly distributed within society, and this could support the transition to socialism.[28] Among many of the Labour Party's parliamentary members prior to the First World War, it became widely accepted that while skilled workers could potentially provide for themselves through receipt of union benefits, poorer union members, as well as unorganized workers, including women, did not have such advantages. Consequently, the state must provide welfare support. And when economic misfortune struck those better-situated workers, they might themselves require support from the state.

Acceptance among labor's parliamentary representatives for a greater role for the state in the provision of welfare emerged within a wider context of increasing working-class assertiveness. Beginning in the final decades of the nineteenth century, the growing presence of labor did not go unnoticed. Moreover, the labor

movement witnessed significant expansion. Crucially, as Vicente
Navarro pointed out, the composition of the British working class
at this time evolved, with the dominance of craft and textile unions
giving way to those representing coal miners, railway workers, and
dockers—sections of the labor force more responsive to socialist ideas. Moreover, the acceptance of a more radical agenda was
encouraged by social unrest rumblings among the working classes
in the rest of Europe, particularly the failed Russian Revolution of
October 1905 and the growth of discontent in Germany. Within
this climate, in conjunction with the party's acceptance of the
state's importance, the early Labour Party warmed to state welfare.
Both unions and the Labour Party enthusiastically endorsed the
idea of non-contributory universal state pensions. Furthermore,
although in part a result of not wanting to be outflanked by the
Liberal government with regard to social reforms, the Labour
Party principally supported the National Insurance Act of 1911 as
a step in the right direction, although it criticized it for not being
redistributive in nature and for failing to adequately support the
poorest members of the labor force.[29]

The Consequences of War

As part of the nation's efforts during the First World War, the role
of the British state in social and economic affairs grew exponentially between 1914 and 1918. Its intervention through government
controls, regulations, and ownership demonstrated the power
of the state to organize society and the economy, and instigate
social change. The war represented for most of the population
an intimate relationship with the state, the likes of which had not
been experienced before. And for many within the labor movement this relationship proved positive. Due to labor shortages
and increasing demands on production, large swathes of civilian workers experienced increased employment opportunities,
economic security, and growth in wages. With organized labor
increasingly embedded within the state apparatus, there emerged

a growing realization among many within the working class of the state's potential to enhance living and working conditions.[30] In the immediate years after 1918 fear prevailed among many within the labor movement that benefits achieved during the war would be lost if there was a return to the prewar environment. As Labour Party politician Arthur Henderson and socialist economist G. D. H. Cole concluded in 1919, having investigated the state of the labor movement, many had discovered that "private profit is not an equitable basis upon which to build."[31]

It is true that the experience of the war did not contribute to the universal acceptance of the state among all within the working-class, with initial attempts by some unions in the years following 1918 to distance themselves from the state. With union membership expanding, along with the increasing influence of labor within industry, a focus upon collective bargaining and "industry solutions" became the preferred means to advance labor's position.[32] Nonetheless, a more intricate relationship with the state had been established, the consequences of which were difficult to repeal. Ralph Miliband observed that within much of the labor movement there was an enthusiastic zeal to retain greater state control on a permanent basis.[33]

The years after the First World War were tumultuous, with an emboldened working class making itself felt. Historian Jane Morgan noted that the period between November 1918 and late 1921 witnessed one of the most prolonged episodes of working-class militancy ever in Britain.[34] With labor militants burning with revolutionary opportunity, and inspired by the Bolshevik Revolution of October 1917, 1919 represented the apex of this disquiet, as ex-servicemen and a war-weary public agitated for radical change. Even prior to the war's end, Prime Minister David Lloyd George asserted, "The whole state of society is more or less molten."[35] For John Saville, "1919 had probably the greatest potential for radical reform. . . . The opening months . . . were a time when a political explosion seemed inevitable" as mutinies within the armed forces occurred alongside waves of strikes in major industries that struck trepidation into the heart of government.[36] Largely supported by the TUC, but with the pressure primarily arising from the rank and file of the union movement, a broad cross section of the working class engaged in industrial action. From the perspective of capital, the situation was so serious that genuine fears of revolution prevailed.

Seizing upon this temperament of revolt and agitation—in the face of the collapse of the Second International—some working-class organizations again argued against utilizing Parliament and the use of reforms. With a British Communist Party yet to be established, many Marxists in the years after the war felt confident to voice their opposition to parliamentary methods, as epitomized by organizations such as the Workers' Socialist Federation, of which Sylvia Pankhurst was the most high-profile member. The zealousness exhibited by some for the rejection of reforms, between 1917 and 1921, Macintyre said, "stemmed from a starry-eyed conviction that the revolution was at hand and therefore that the 'parliamentary machine' was as good as obsolete."[37] Despite the exuberance by some for such a method, the prewar position was soon reasserted by Lenin in the pages of *Left-Wing Communism: An Infantile Disorder.* Here, Lenin was openly critical of those who were opposed to engaging with Parliament, asserting that it remained politically relevant as part of a wider revolutionary strategy. While opposition to Parliament may be necessary at times, this was very much dependant on the situation. A complete rejection of Parliament, Lenin firmly asserted, was foolish.

The animosity and rancor pervading the rank and file of the labor movement infiltrated the Labour Party. In a more coherent shift to the left compared to the years prior to the First World War, by 1918 Labour had positioned itself as a proletarian alternative to the Liberal and Conservative parties. In the early months of that year, with overwhelming support from its membership, clause IV of the party's constitution was introduced, which endeavored to "secure for the workers by hand or by brain the full fruits of their industry and the most equitable distribution thereof that may be possible, upon the basis of the common ownership of the means of production."[38] In proposing a radical working-class agenda, the Labour Party embraced the state as the vehicle through which to regulate capitalism and implement its socialist values. This was evident no more so than in the party's publication, *Labour and the New Social Order: A Report on Reconstruction.*

Indicative of a more positive attitude by the labor movement toward the state, the Labour Party called for the common ownership of land as soon as opportunity arose, as well as the immediate nationalization of railways, canals, coal mines, electricity, and the manufacturers and proprietors of alcohol. State intervention and regulations were also proposed to ensure that minimum standards would be maintained in relation to wages, health, and education. The state was also to guarantee employment opportunities and increase economic demand to support jobs and the availability of work. Moreover, municipal government would be revitalized. Integral to social reconstruction, the state would continue to have responsibility for services such as sanitation, water, gas, and education, along with an expanded role in housing and town planning, public recreation such as leisure facilities, and the distribution and coordination of milk.

Economic Decline

Economic stagnation emerged during the early 1920s, resulting in the escalation of severe unemployment. Affecting many skilled members of the working class, organized labor increasingly looked to the state for assistance. The state had a role to play in combating the oppression and exploitation of the labor force, an understanding shared throughout much of the labor movement, including within its more radical Marxist wings. Lenin's reassertion that parliamentary activity was vital infused the position of the Communist International, which replaced the Second International in 1919. While its membership was less varied than that of the Second International, it nevertheless retained an adherence to parliamentary methods, as well as more direct action, including armed struggle, for the abolition of capitalism. At its Third Congress, in 1921, it was explicitly stated that no genuine long-term improvement in the position of labor could be achieved under capitalism. However, this did not mean that "the proletariat has to renounce the fight for its immediate practical demands until after it has established its dictatorship." The Congress forcefully asserted that Communist parties must put forward, and fight for, demands that represent the immediate needs and interests of labor.[39] At the start of the 1920s, it was thus the case that a broad consensus emerged within the labor movement, one in which the capitalist state, social reforms, and bourgeois democratic institutions continued to be identified as central to the class struggle, and as a means to combat oppression and exploitation.

In Britain economic security was the dominant issue of concern for labor as the war ended, stimulating efforts to press the state for welfare support. An increasing number of unions forcefully argued for an expansion of state unemployment support, with more radical groups agitating for a permanent, generous, non-contributory scheme, which had been introduced on a temporary basis after the Armistice to support the increasing numbers of the unemployed due to the ending of wartime production and demobilization. In response, the government hastily introduced unemployment reforms in 1920. These reforms were characterized by an increase in the amount of unemployment benefits under the insurance system.[40]

That working-class attitudes during the 1920s were evolving more favorably toward state welfare was also exemplified by the actions of those municipalities under the authority of more radical elements of the labor movement. An example was the administrative actions of Poplar, a district of East London. Stimulated in part by the expansion of the franchise, which resulted in the election of many socialist-inspired labor representatives, Poplar came to symbolize the defiance of labor. Among its policies was the enthusiastic construction of muncipial housing, a free milk scheme for expectant mothers and babies, the appointment of a tuberculosis officer, and the expansion of library services and public park recreational facilities.[41] Identified as "Poplarism," it was not a spontaneous act of the poor, but rather the culmination of careful and sustained socialist organization embedded within its working-class community.[42]

The use of the municipal state by the workforce of Poplar was characterized by generous rates of unemployment relief above minimum wage levels, eschewing the pressure to consider the full earnings of a family when offering support, as well as providing unemployment assistance for those engaged in industrial disputes.[43] While Poplar came to symbolize this process, similar actions occurred in other parts of Britain where more radical members of the labor movement had been elected to local government by their communities. Such cases exemplify how a combination of working-class pressure and elected socialist representatives culminated in the acceptance of the state as a positive instrument to support the welfare needs of the working class. The actions of Poplar and other radical municipal authorities echoed the position adopted by the Second International prior to the war. This is shown by a resolution passed in 1900 that asserted: "It is the duty of all socialists . . . to make clear to all the value of municipal activity . . . to endeavor to municipalize such public services as the urban transport service, education, shops, bakeries, medical assistance, hospitals, water supply, baths and washhouses . . . dwellings for the people . . . to see that these public services shall be model services."[44]

Throughout the 1920s and 1930s, as economic stagnation came to characterize much of the British economy, acceptance by the working class of the potential advantages of state welfare support gradually became solidified within the labor movement. As mass unemployment impeded both union benefits and state insurance schemes that were underpinned by contributions from both labor and capital, many within the labor movement turned their attention to non-contributory universal state support. Reflecting an evolving position during the 1920s, the TUC fully endorsed the expansion of health and unemployment benefits, and was openly hostile to reduced benefit rates, restrictions on access, and expressed opposition to the contributory principle.[45] With collective bargaining diminishing in influence, organized labor orientated itself to engaging with the state to stimulate advancements to enhance working-class material conditions, with state welfare central to this.

Undeniably, the acceptance of state welfare by the mainstream labor movement emerged during a period of weakness. With some accuracy it could be claimed that the working class initially was, at best, ambivalent about state welfare. However, economic decline, unemployment, and reduced opportunity for collective bargaining during the 1920s and 1930s contributed significantly to the labor movement accepting state support in relation to unemployment, and then, gradually, in relation to other aspects of welfare. On this basis, it can be said that the labor movement, rather than actively pursuing state welfare support, resigned itself to accepting the state as the movement's only source of leverage and resistance. However, an alternative position, one that more accurately reflects the dialectical relationship between the working class, welfare state, and capitalism, is that labor accepted and pursued the need for state welfare as material conditions changed. As the conditions of accumulation evolved so did the context in which the class struggle was fought. Labor, adjusting to declining economic growth, adapted itself to political and economic conditions in which state welfare provision existed in embryonic form. In this process, much of the labor movement evolved to accept a greater role for the state as part of the wider class struggle, and as such adapted to the existence of state welfare as an instrument to be used in their continuing opposition to capital.

6

Social Security

More explicitly than other welfare services, social security systems, which include services providing cash support by the state for, among other situations—old-age, unemployment, long-term sickness, and disability—embody capitalist social relations.[1] Influenced by the socio-historical nature of class conflict, the class struggle permeates the organization of these services. Social security exists as an institution of a capitalist state whose objective is the long-term preservation of capitalism. But the state operates within a wider context of class struggle, reflecting the conflict between subordinate groups and their oppressors. Analogous with Engels's arguments regarding the state as an apparatus of capitalism, social security is a welfare service that reflects the irreconcilable antagonisms between labor and capital.[2]

Although parsimonious in nature, social security offers valuable basic support to labor. Its inclusion within working-class struggles over the last century testifies to this.[3] But, equally, it has been seized upon by capital for having the purpose of enforcing wage labor. Under capitalism, social security has come to constitute a significant instrument of coercion. It regulates the working class and ensures that the social relations between capital and labor remain one of capital's domination. Capital, although frequently demonstrating caution, and often outright hostility, has utilized it as a method to buttress its hegemonic dominance.

Reflecting upon social security reforms implemented in Britain during the 2010s, which occurred within the context of public sector austerity, this chapter will exemplify the extent to which social security is organized and shaped by the requirements of capitalism. However, rather than accepting a one-sided interpretation of the complex and dialectical nature of welfare services, this chapter will demonstrate how social security systems have been embraced by the working class for protection from exploitation and oppression.

Social Security and the Reproduction of Labor

Social security is frequently the object of vehement criticism from capital. Anxiety abounds concerning its potential perversion of society's morals, that it discourages work, and potentially incites the working class to eschew wage labor altogether. For capital, that a system exists allowing individuals to acquire financial support without having to enter the labor market threatens the foundation of capitalism itself. Social security is often regarded with suspicion and hesitancy; however, this should not obscure the fact that it offers various benefits to capital. It occupies a central role supporting the reproduction of labor, reproducing in full, or in part, the material conditions of many members of the labor force.[4] Furthermore, it is essential to facilitating the development of a broad capitalist morality in terms of attitudes and behavior, thus supporting the commodification of labor power. From the perspective of capital, social security constitutes a powerful instrument regulating the lives of many of society's most disadvantaged and vulnerable groups to ensure their reproduction as labor power. Fundamental to this role is the reproduction of non-working members of the population.

For varying reasons some individuals are exempt from the labor market, such as children, the elderly, long-term sick, those who are considered disabled, and the unemployed. Many, however, are likely to enter the labor force at some point. And when they are not working, they constitute members of the reserve army of labor.[5] For Marx the reserve army has the role of regulating the existing labor force, significantly as a mechanism to restrain wage growth as members of the labor force may moderate their demands if they feel they can be replaced by others waiting to take their jobs.[6] Marx identified an eclectic group of individuals who make up this surplus group of workers. The most significant categories of the reserve army of labor identified by Marx, which remain acutely relevant at present, include those labeled as floating and stagnant members. The floating population consists of those who are unemployed because of the normal business cycle but are searching for work. Stagnant members are defined by irregular part-time and casual employment, resulting in reduced labor market skills and a material existence below the average of the working-class. Additionally, Marx identified "the lowest sediment of the relative surplus-population" as those who exist in a state of pauperism.[7] Despite severe pockets of poverty in many advanced capitalist nations, it is the case that this last category remains particularly applicable to the nations of the Global South.

To restrain wage growth, and for the labor market to operate in the interests of capital, it is vital to have a plentiful supply of floating members of the reserve army of labor. They are closest to the labor market at any one time in terms of actively seeking work and being prepared for it. Yet it is imperative that such individuals have their ability and willingness to labor maintained when outside of the labor market, and social security is central to this. It is integral to maintaining workers' material conditions so that they display the sufficient physical and mental attributes required when they are working. Additionally, social security has an ideological function. reinforcing the acceptance of the need to work. Furthermore, social security can go some way to supporting recipients' ability to acquire appropriate, albeit often basic, skills required by the labor market.

Sustaining Material Need

Although limited in monetary terms, social security payments offer social groups a vital source of income, one they would unlikely obtain otherwise. This allows for the opportunity to purchase use values and largely guarantees the availability of essential commodities. Modestly securing the material reproduction of non-working individuals, this process is instrumental to producing future wage laborers. The income transferred helps to ensure that their physical and mental capacity to labor is maintained. However, material conditions supported by social security must always be at a level that acts as an incentive for those receiving support to opt for wage labor instead of opposing it. For capital the material existence of non-working groups is a matter of significant political and economic concern. Social security represents the means through which the political apparatus of advanced capitalist societies intervenes in their lives to regulate living conditions and ensure, while they are fit to work, that their experience of life outside of the labor market is one that encourages work.

Regulating material support offered by social security permeated welfare reforms introduced in Britain during the 2010s. Rather than providing social security benefits measured against the Retail Price Index (RPI), which includes housing costs, reforms introduced, which remain in place today, set benefit levels to increase by the Consumer Price Index (CPI), which excludes housing costs. This curtailed the rate at which benefits rise. Moreover, for three years, starting in 2013, most working-age benefits and in-work support programs were limited to a below inflation increase of 1 percent per annum. Additionally, in 2016, rates for the same programs were frozen for four more years at 2015–16 levels. One of the most momentous reforms was the imposition in 2013 of a household benefit cap, imposing a ceiling on what individuals and families could receive from the state per year. As of mid-2024, the benefit cap amounted to a maximum of £22,020 (about $28,108) for the majority of families each year, and £14,753 for the majority of single individuals (about $18,832).[8]

Attempting to consolidate class relations, reductions to benefits were made as part of wider efforts to bolster the supply of labor under conditions of economic stagnation. The British government made little effort to conceal its agenda, which was to coerce individuals into accepting wage labor or face destitution. As the then Minister for Welfare Reform, Lord Freud, asserted in 2011: "The benefit cap provides a clear, simple message . . . to achieve positive effects through changed attitudes to welfare, responsible life choices and strong work incentives."[9]

Social security must be understood as an essential mechanism aiding the creation of the working class. As a system, it is integral to managing individuals to actively offer their labor power as a commodity. Intervention in the lives of non-working groups, providing income support at an appropriate level to ensure their physical and mental condition, is vital in the transformation from what sociologist Claus Offe described as "passive proletarianization," a situation of non-wage labor, to "active proletarianization" whereby individuals are engaged in the labor process.[10] Yet the existence of sufficient material conditions constitutes only one element social security plays in constituting wage labor. The management of behavior and the generation of appropriate attitudes are essential to the purpose of social security.

Social Control and Labor Discipline

Labor power is the possession of a living, thoughtful, and reflective human being.[11] And it is because of this that its reproduction is both necessary and challenging. "The maintenance and reproduction of labour . . . is not just a question of the physical reproduction of a class," social work scholars Chris Jones and Tony Novak wrote, "it is also a political reproduction which creates a class that is both able and willing to work."[12] Reproduction of class relations is greatly dependent upon the nurturing of a capitalist morality of attitudes and actions, exemplified by labor expressing docility, discipline, and obedience.

The fear that social security may pervert the work ethic and encourage attitudes and behaviors in opposition to those thought beneficial to capitalism underpinned British welfare reforms during the 2010s. The then Conservative prime minister, David Cameron, made this clear, arguing, "For years we've had a system that encourages the worst in people—that incites laziness . . . that erodes self-discipline, that discourages hard work . . . people thinking they can be as irresponsible as they like because the state will always bail them out."[13] Here, Cameron was echoing the fears and hostility of many politicians and members of capital, who have identified social security provisions as a potential threat to capitalist social relations. In response to this fear, capital has been motivated to impose itself upon social security and embrace it as a mechanism of social control to ensure that people are available as wage labor. In the economic context of the 2010s, with stagnation prevailing in the aftermath of the Great Financial Crisis of 2007–2009, the necessity to intensify the exploitation of labor, as well as ensure the growth of its availability, was seized upon as essential to stimulating economic expansion.

An Instrument of Ideology

Among all social security reforms in Britain during the 2010s, the introduction of Universal Credit (UC) was instrumental for enforcing the hegemonic dominance of capitalism and a capitalist morality. Underpinning this was the aim of imposing upon recipients an ethic of wage labor. Fundamental to UC was establishing conditions of claiming and an experience of receiving that mirrors life within the labor market. A paramount ideological objective is to ensure that relying upon social security reflects the experiences of active members of the labor force and promotes a labor market culture.

Mirroring a dominant characteristic of the labor market, UC is paid monthly in order to encourage recipients to acquire the skills of managing a monthly budget. In addition, UC aims to reflect the labor process by constructing the relationship between claimant and the program itself as a contract. Just as employees are contractually obliged to fulfill their labor market role, so claimants have a duty to pursue work in return for state support. "Deliberately mirroring a contract of employment," the government has argued, "the Claimant Commitment makes clear that welfare is no different from work itself. Just as those in work have obligations to their employer, so too claimants have a responsibility to the taxpayer."[14] Central to this "contractual" obligation is the active pursuit of work, either through identifying employment or engaging in work-based training. A failure to fulfil this obligation can result in sanctions amounting to a loss of benefit for up to three years. Furthermore, it has been asserted that searching for work must be viewed as work itself, as claimants should consider themselves "in work to find work."[15] Again, the work ethic characterizes all aspects of UC's delivery and the experience of receiving it, an attempt to instill and foster among claimants values and behavior that support a labor market morality.

At the heart of UC has been an effort to promote an ideology that reinforces the work ethic.. The recipients of UC, particularly those who are members of the reserve army of labor, must possess attributes that present them as employable. Within many advanced capitalist nations, eligibility for social security is constituted upon recipients actively participating in work-based initiatives, such as training and voluntary work, demonstrating they are pursing work and developing relevant labor market skills. Active engagement in labor market–related activity is fundamentally an effort to promote attitudes, skills, and behavior that cultivates labor discipline. This facilitates the creation of a compliant source of potential labor that possesses the skills required for, and accepts the inevitability of, work.

Wage Levels and Subsidization

Much of the focus here has been on the relationship between social security and non-working members of society. But, as a welfare service, it also has implications for individuals already employed. Social security contributes greatly to reducing the costs to capital of the reproduction of many active members of the labor force.[16] Commonly below average working-class wages, social security rates constitute a base against which the minimum value of labor is established. Wages, particularly at the bottom of the labor market, must not fall below the rate of benefits, particularly unemployment benefits, to encourage individuals to accept work. The lower the rate of benefit, the lower minimum wage rates can be set, but always they should not fall below the rate of benefit. Social security programs define the benchmark against which minimum wages must compete.

As well as helping to determine wage rates, social security also subsidizes wages.[17] To reduce the costs to capital of employing low-wage labor, in-work benefits are commonly provided by many social security systems within the advanced capitalist nations. The subsidization of wages, allowing individuals to work and claim benefits, affords them a greater opportunity to purchase goods that contribute to their material reproduction. Yet, for capital, the advantage of in-work benefits is that they can diminish the burden of labor's reproduction by reducing the incentive to increase wages if the state intervenes to make up the shortfall.

The subsidization of wages can be illustrated with reference again to UC. Between 2016 and 2022, approximately 42 percent of all UC recipients were employed.[18] The amount of UC workers are eligible to receive depends on the amount they earn, with it reduced as their earnings increase. There is no minimum or maximum number of hours individuals can work and receive UC simultaneously. For claimants this is undoubtedly attractive, viewing their wages as topped-up by the state. However, government has been candid regarding the advantages this has for employers, arguing UC "creates a flexible workforce that helps employers grow their business."[19] Confronted with a supply of labor in a position to work as many hours as is required to be profitable employers have the flexibility to maintain wages at a reduced rate while the state subsidizes labor's income.

A Dialectical Object of Class Struggle

Up to this point the argument is that social security must be considered crucial to support the reproduction of capitalist social relations and to solidify working-class oppression. This was exemplified clearly with reforms to the welfare system in Britain throughout the 2010s. But despite this it is too simplistic, and one-dimensional, to leave the analysis there. Emblematic of the contradictory nature of welfare provision, social security cannot simply be understood as a weapon of capital's domination and exploitation alone.

To understand social security systems within the context of advanced capitalism, including their history, it must be acknowledged they offer benefits to labor, even if considerable criticism can be made of their punitive nature. Monetary benefits do ensure an element of protection against the unpredictability of the market. Like the welfare state itself, social security is not a monolithic institution imposing capital's will upon the working class. Rather, its origins can be found in class struggle, with this providing the context for the historical, and present, organization of social security systems. Exemplifying this contradiction, there exists considerable evidence to prove that the working class have championed the same social security systems to defend itself from oppression and exploitation as has been used by capital to instigate exploitation and oppression.

Lenin on Social Security

The radical implications of social security for the working class were initially identified by Lenin. While Marx and Engels provide little in the way of direct commentary applicable to an analysis of social security, we can turn to Lenin for a possible understanding of how it could support the working class as part of the class struggle. Prior to the Russian Revolution of 1917, Lenin enthusiastically accepted the provision of social security as part of his wider method of fighting for socialism, which involved using the parliamentary system to advance reforms. These reforms were proclaimed as beneficial for both the immediate alleviation of working-class exploitation as well as for raising class consciousness. Asserting his position in 1912, Lenin made clear that a socialist social security system should provide unemployment, old age, illness, accident, disability, maternity, and bereavement support. Such a system would provide benefits equal to wages, covering all wage-earners and their families. Envisioning it as a state insurance system, Lenin recognized it should be funded by both employers and the state. Moreover, the administration should be firmly in the hands of workers.

Critical of a proposed social security reform bill passing through the Russian Duma at the time, Lenin urged the working class to oppose it, arguing, "The main point of this agitation should be to explain to the proletarian masses that no real improvement in the worker's conditions is possible unless there is a new revolutionary upsurge, that whoever wishes to achieve a genuine labour reform must above all fight for a new, victorious revolution."[20] Yet Lenin also made clear that should the bill become law workers must agitate for its expansion and utilize it. They should recast the law "into a means of developing its class-consciousness, strengthening its organization and intensifying its struggle for full political liberty and for socialism."[21] From Lenin's account state welfare reforms were something that, though utilized by capital, were central to working-class concerns. State social security, rather than a weapon solely wielded by capital, was a potential platform upon which the class struggle could be fought. It was a vital foundation for workers to advance their immediate interests, as well as the long-term goals of socialism.

Reform and the Fear of Revolution

Mirroring Lenin's support for social security reforms, social security's centrality to the labor movement in the advanced capitalist nations in the years prior to the First World War was epitomized by the resolutions of the Second International between 1889 and 1916. With welfare reforms figuring prominently within the life of the Second International, consistent with Lenin's position resolutions proposing state-sponsored insurance covering sickness, health, old age, maternity, and unemployment were passed. These reforms were considered essential for both the immediate interests of labor as well as supporting the long-term fight for revolutionary change.[22]

As was made clear in the last chapter, in Britain, the years between 1919 and 1921 witnessed significant bouts of unrest by the labor movement which were often violent in nature. Despite a brief and immediate postwar boom, Britain's position within the world economy had severe consequences for many of its heavy industries. Coal mining, steel making, and shipbuilding, which had been highly dependent on overseas trade prior to the war, experienced decline in the years afterward as global capitalist activity stagnated. This was exacerbated by the trend for protectionist policies and tariffs. As trade fell so did the flow of capital. In those areas with a high concentration of heavy industry, such as Wales, Scotland, and northern England, unemployment mushroomed, with the average rate rarely falling below 10 percent for well over a decade.[23]

With economic decline and rising unemployment, fear of revolution spread among the ranks of capital. Within government, historian Bentley B. Gilbert observed that there was "fear of popular violence if something was not done to provide security for the British working man."[24] Building upon the existing unemployment insurance scheme, introduced in 1911 largely in response to the growing assertiveness of the working class, labor was once again victorious, nearly a decade later, in wresting concessions from the Liberal government. With discontent spreading throughout working-class communities up and down the country in the after-math of the war, and fear spreading among the ruling class, the government increased benefit levels, reduced the amount work-ers were expected to contribute, as well as expanding the number of occupations eligible to join the scheme. Nonetheless, protests continued.

By early 1921 unemployment continued to be an urgent threat to social stability. There remained over 300,000 ex-servicemen unemployed. Fear swelled within government as to their collective potential, with outbursts of violence in major cities throughout Britain. Moreover, there existed the continuing threat posed by many civilian unemployed, with sustained outbreaks of disruption sporadically characterizing working-class communities. Again, consternation among labor was that the rate of benefit was insuf-ficient to maintain an unemployed worker and their family. Acting on fear, not only did the government enhance the rate of payment for the individual who was unemployed but also, for the first time, provided additional payments for dependents, including children. Direct action by labor in response to uncertain economic condi-tions, the fear of being buffeted by the dictates of the market, and the desire for greater security of income greatly influenced the expansion of social security provision, as the working class seized upon it as a means of resisting oppression and combating exploita-tion and destitution.

Disability Protest and Social Security

In possibly the bleakest period for working people in the whole of the twentieth century, during much of the 1920s and 1930s the fight for increased unemployment support was central, not just to the class struggle, but to the survival of the working class. With unemployment spreading, this did not mean the working class was a spent force. Certainly, in these years defeats were experi-enced, but both decades witnessed victories. The actions of the labor movement, and crucially the establishment of the National

Unemployed Worker's Movement (NUWM), as well as the electoral advancement of more radical representatives of the working class within municipal government, enhanced working-class strength. In those regions where the labor movement was strong, local unemployment support, though not generous, was nevertheless implemented and provided more sympathetically, and often more generously, than in regions of weaker resistance.[25]

Working-class support for state social security continued after the Second World War in terms of the expansion in the number of benefits and provision of state support as a right.[26] Moreover, throughout the relative affluence of the postwar boom, during the 1960s and 1970s, social security provision proliferated. Reflecting the system's contradictions, it is certainly the case that the number of benefits grew in response to the needs of capitalism. But the pressures of the labor movement, as well as interest groups representing various vulnerable members of society, also influenced this expansion. Governments throughout this period tried to manage this growth in favor of it having as little negative consequence for capitalism as possible but recognizing the influence of working people.[27]

Although met with mixed results, expressions of resistance characterized many among the working class as benefits were cut in the 1980s and 1990s. The neoliberal assault on Britain during this era continued into the early 2000s, and culminated in the era of welfare retrenchment during the 2010s. As already discussed in this chapter, this period witnessed a significant attack upon the British social security system. Yet it also stimulated noble efforts of resistance. Almost a century after the working class won vital social security reforms in the aftermath of the First World War, the importance of social security for protection against the instability and exploitation of the free market was once again apparent. The capitalist assault on benefits was challenged forcefully, this time with the disability movement at its heart. An analysis of disability will be the focus of the next chapter, but the actions of radical disability rights activists were significant in trying to both oppose the increasingly oppressive nature of the British social security system and ensure that it offered an element of support that freed individuals from exploitation. Experiencing reductions in welfare support of nearly £5 billion between 2010 and 2021, with a further £7 billion of reductions to municipal government services, many individuals with disabilities united to combat attacks on their living conditions. The levels of oppression felt resulted in disability activists positioning themselves at the heart of the wider anti-austerity movement during the 2010s.[28]

From the outset, championing the cause of all disabled individuals was Disabled People Against Cuts (DPAC), who, as co-founder Bob Williams-Findlay argued, embraced a radical materialist anticapitalist agenda.[29] Reflecting the desire for radical social change, but accepting the value of reforms under capitalism to support this, for DPAC the root cause of oppression was located within the operation of capitalist society. Reductions to the provision of existing state welfare would exacerbate this oppression. Their fight was aimed at reforming the existing system, while recognizing that real change would only come with the transformation of society's social structures. With the exploitation of disabled individuals derived from capitalist social relations, DPAC pursued alliances with trade unions, as well as the wider anti-austerity movement.[30]

Among other campaigns, one notable effort to oppose the use of social security to intensify the exploitation of labor was DPACs resistance to "workfare" policies. Eligibility for social security support for the disabled was, as it remains, based upon accepting a position on work-related schemes. Compulsory work placement programs, often within the private sector, meant claimants received no pay and lasted anywhere from four weeks to six months. The assertion by government was that these programs would enhance an individual's employability, equipping them with the skills and experience required to get work. Yet evidence indicated the impact of the programs was negligible.[31]

During the initial phase of workfare programs, many national-based retail outlets took advantage of it, utilizing it as a method to meet seasonal temporary demand rather than hiring paid workers. Met with fierce resistance, DPAC, alongside other anti-austerity organizations, campaigned tirelessly, opposing these schemes of forced labor. Protests were organized, among them occupations of the retail outlets of many of the corporate participants. Fearing for their public reputation, prominent retail chains began to abandon the various workfare programs. In the case of one leading supermarket chain, after protesters occupied several of their stores, which garnered public attention, claimants were offered wages. Following this, the number of available placements had significantly declined, and by 2014 the program was discontinued as more private sector organizations withdrew their support.

Although unable to reverse reductions to social security rates, DPAC's efforts exemplified the centrality of social security for the lives of many within the labor movement. Their actions made explicit that the same system that can be utilized by capitalism to oppress them also constitutes a vital source of support and defense against the ravages of the market.

Social Security and Socialism

This chapter has gone some way to illustrate the contradictory nature of social security under capitalism. Undoubtedly, social security systems commonly have been less than generous in nature and punitive in their operation. They have enforced strict eligibility criteria and intervened significantly in people's lives. But they have offered members of the wider population a minimum level of protection against complete destitution and a source of income obtainable outside of the direct exploitation and oppression of the workplace. The position of Lenin, the Second International, as well as the history of working-class action, indicate that the advancement and protection of existing social security systems within the context of capitalism has been, and remains, essential to workers as part of the class struggle.

Social security systems, within the context of advanced

capitalism, are not just instruments of capital. They are platforms of class conflict. Although an institution of a capitalist state, the historical reality of the state under capitalism is that there have been periods and events when its organizational form and actions have been influenced by labor. As indicated in chapter 2, sociologist Sean Damer asserted, the state is the "cockpit of class struggle" with its structure "the outcome, the expression, of class struggle."[32] Additionally, as Jennifer Dale said, the state is an expression of class power, with its structure and functioning determined, on the one hand, by capital's attempt to reproduce its dominance, and on the other, labor's efforts to combat its exploitation.[33] Social security exemplifies this. Its very existence evolved from the class struggle, with capital recognizing its introduction as imperative to quell working-class agitation, but also accepting the benefits it would have for economic growth. The working-class, however, saw social security as a mechanism to protect them against the raw harshness of the labor market. Its evolution since has subsequently reflected the struggle between capital and labor, with both identifying it as essential to advancing their interests.

From the perspective of the working class, it can be claimed that social security systems offer the foundations of an alternative system of socialist income support. For sure, evolving under capitalism means in their current form they are far from perfect, but they do, nevertheless, offer the seeds of something that is anti-capitalist in nature, being comparable to Marx's understanding of cooperatives, when he stated they represented "within the old form the first sprouts of the new, although they naturally reproduce . . . all the shortcomings of the prevailing system."[34] Largely supporting this principle, as Michael Lebowitz contends, existing capitalism does not just contain institutions and value systems that benefit capitalism only. Capitalist society contains alternative organizations reflecting anti-capitalist values, which offer an alternative way forward.[35]

Social security systems offer an elementary vision of a source of income, and a means of obtaining financial support, that does not rely upon being a member of the workforce. Primarily operated by and delivered through the state, social security depicts the basis of a collective method of income provision. It provides the seeds of an alternative anti-capitalist income system, one that illustrates the potential of universal income sources, provided to everyone as a right. Under socialism, and as part of the transition period from capitalism, social security systems could feasibly evolve to form universal basic income (UBI) systems. Replacing social security systems altogether, they would offer a guaranteed income level for all that is not related to work, and subsequently help to break the link between exploitation and oppression on the one hand, and survival and a meaningful existence on the other.

7

Disability

Beyond the COVID pandemic of 2020–21, the global burden of communicable diseases has declined. Non-communicable conditions such as strokes, cardiovascular disease, and chronic obstructive pulmonary disease have increased, however, and have contributed to the growing prevalence of disability. In 2017, an estimated 80 percent of all disabilities globally were caused by non-communicable diseases, with lower-back pain, headaches, and depressive disorders the leading causes.[1] By 2023, approximately 16 percent of the world's population had a disability, amounting to 1.3 billion people with functional difficulties.[2]

Following the biomedical model, disability is frequently conceptualized as a biological phenomenon and equated with impairment. Irrefutably, many individuals experience impairments that restrict their lives, and it would be churlish to deny the real benefits medical interventions have made to alleviating distress. Yet it would be a mistake to perceive all such individuals as inherently disabled.

Over four decades ago, the Union of the Physically Impaired Against Segregation, an organization of socialist-inspired British disability activists, argued that a distinction must be made between impairment and disability.[3] In this, disability must be understood as a social concept depicting the oppression and exclusion experienced by individuals with impairments.[4] Originating from the socioeconomic conditions of capitalism, disability is a social status predicated upon the incompatibility between the corporeal functionality of an individual with an impairment and the requirements of the production process.

A historical-materialist analysis of the relationship between disability, the body, and capitalism must be understood in order to develop a Marxist understanding of disability. Although neither Marx nor Engels specifically theorized disability, a Marxist analysis can be identified within their work, one that explicitly allows us to define disability against the needs and requirements of the production process. Drawing upon changes to disability policy in Britain during the 2010s, capital has explicitly seized upon welfare policy aimed at disabled individuals, specifically income-maintenance policy, to determine who is both able-bodied and disabled. The welfare state is employed as an instrument to define who is considered able-bodied or disabled, making policy to measure and identify an individual's ability to work. If defined as having the ability to work, a person is subsequently not considered disabled. However, despite disability welfare policy having been used against the disabled, in many cases to enhance their exploitation and oppression, it is also the case that disability campaigns to protect welfare services have been significant. Exemplifying the class struggles encompassing the welfare state, the actions of these activists, as well as earlier historical examples from British history, show that working-class disabled individuals have fought for welfare provisions and support for more than a century. The same institution that enforced their oppression has also been identified as instrumental in combating this oppression.

Marx and Engels: The Body and Capitalism

Under capitalism, disability is considered an inherent biological characteristic of individuals who have physical, cognitive, or mental health impairments resulting in limited functioning relative to "normal." Conceptions of able-bodied and disabled, influenced by the biomedical model, are determined by notions of biological normality and understandings of physiological acceptability. Disability and impairment are generally constructed as interchangeable. However, from a Marxist perspective, a distinction exists between impairment and disability. Impairment refers to a real phenomenon. It is the physical, cognitive, and mental health challenges an individual might experience. Disability, however, is a social status as a result of impairment excluding people from work. While accepting the existence of impairment as a biological reality, it is important to recognize that the single most significant determinant of disability is the organization of the mode of production based on the maximization of profit. Economic exploitation contributes greatly to determining who is disabled and able-bodied.[5] For capital, labor power is the source of value. Thus, bodies that can be exploited in the labor process are paramount. The inability to work is instrumental in identifying individuals considered disabled. Disability is a status representing the social and economic disadvantages experienced by those with impairments. The most prominent reason for this is an incompatibility between their corporeality and the requirements of exploitative wage labor. By this we mean that under capitalism an individual is disabled, not because of their impairment, but because they are excluded from the labor process. Their impairment precludes them from being part of the labor force as their body does not fit the requirements of work under capitalism. Disability, therefore, is a social and economic status symbolizing the marginalization and exclusion of those who have this label imposed upon them.

Neither Marx nor Engels developed a theory of disability, although the origins of one can be identified within their analysis of the relationship between capitalism and the body. Labor, Marx contended, is a corporeal phenomenon requiring the "exertion of the bodily organs" with the laborer setting "in motion arms and legs, head and hands, the natural forces of his body."[6] The labor process dictates bodily actions, which, in turn, greatly determine what type of bodily capacity is required to function within the labor market. This gives rise to the idea of a normative bodily capacity, with individuals having to possess a particular corporeal potential to function as part of the labor force, operating as "conscious organs" that "co-ordinate with the unconscious organs of the automation."[7] Capital subsequently imposes conditions upon workers, with their bodies having to adapt to the tempo, demands, and expectations of the labor process. Workers synchronize their own movements "to the uniform and unceasing motion of an automation."[8] In this shift, "the machine makes use of him [the worker] . . . it is the movements of the machine that he must follow."[9]

Expectation of a correspondence between corporeal ability and operational needs of the labor process, nonetheless, engenders a possible antagonistic relationship between body and machine if bodily capabilities do not conform to the means of production and labor process. Invoking the concept of "weak bodies," Marx was adamant that the profitability of the means of production was constrained by the limitations of the normative human body.[10] Representing a clash between natural biological "givens" and science, the material composition and corporeal capacity of the body restricts productivity, preventing workers from maintaining pace with the full potential of the productive process. The means of production may go on producing indefinitely, being a possible source of perpetual motion and production, but only if not met "with certain natural obstructions in the weak bodies and the strong wills of its human attendants."[11]

The implications of Marx's position is that workers whose corporeal capacity varies from the standards of the normative body can be considered an obstacle to the production process. From this emerges the notion of some bodies having less economic value than others. Accordingly, the social exclusion of many disabled individuals is firmly grounded within capitalism's rejection of them as a source of economic value. As Marta Russell declares: "A primary basis of oppression of disabled persons . . . is their exclusion from exploitation as wage laborers."[12]

Although not investigating disability, Marx and Engels did not avoid the issue of impairment. Passionately, they denounced how production inflicted physical degradation upon the laboring masses, arguing that the scars of the class struggle lay bare on the bodies of the working class. For Marx, capitalism, "squanders human lives . . . and not only blood and flesh, but also nerve and brain."[13] Attentive observation of this was made by Engels, who witnessed the direct suffering capitalism wreaked upon the body.[14] Integrating the body with the operational requirements of the labor process, impairments were considered customary. Frequent bending and stooping, which characterized factory production, resulted in deformities of workers' backs, shoulders, and knees.[15] Industrialization, Engels stated, contributes to "multitudes of accidents of more or less serious nature, which have for the operative the secondary effect of unfitting him for his work more or less completely."[16] Impairment reduces the ability to labor and acts as a barrier to its sale .When workers' use value as a form of labor is reduced, they are in less demand as a source of economic exploitation. Here, the basis of a Marxist understanding of disability is laid further. Engels depicts the economic and social exclusion individuals with impairments may experience. Marx stressed that individuals with impairments joined the ranks of the reserve army of labor, unable to work, and their existence was largely of pauperism.[17] Described as "demoralised" and "ragged," they were, for Marx, physical victims of capitalist production.[18]

The fact that the conditions of production contribute to the emergence of disability is indisputable. Importantly, the capitalist state is instrumental in reinforcing and solidifying the status of disabled. Acting against a background whereby disabled and able-bodied is significantly determined by notions of the economically exploitable body, the political apparatus of monopoly capitalist society intervenes with social policies that are intrinsic to defining who is, and is not, disabled. Primarily through the welfare system, the state directly imposes upon individuals the category of disabled, or alternatively, the state denies that status, against an assessment of an individual's ability to labor and the requirements of production.

Disability and Dependency under Capitalism

Facing exclusion from the labor process, disabled individuals are likely to require social support. From October to December 2023, an estimated 5.6 percent of disabled people in Britain were unemployed, compared to 3.6 percent of non-disabled. Additionally, a further 42.6 percent were economically inactive. Thus they were not in work or actively seeking it, in comparison to 14.9 percent of non-disabled individuals. In total, 54.2 percent of working-age disabled people in Britain were in work compared to 82.0 percent of non-disabled individuals.[19] The result of high rates of worklessness is that material deprivation pervades the experience of disability. In 2016, during the peak of the British government's austerity drive, an estimated 25 percent of working-age disabled individuals in Britain were considered to live in "deep" poverty, existing on an income below 50 percent of the median, in comparison to 13 percent of non-disabled people.[20] Moreover, in 2022–23, of all families in Britain living in relative low income, after housing costs, 43 percent had at least one member who was disabled.[21]

With exclusion from the labor market and poverty characterizing life for many disabled people, dependency becomes a means of survival. Relative to the often negative attitudes toward social groups not in work, disabled individuals are ordinarily accepted as deserving of social support, although, without doubt, negative portrayals in the media are not uncommon, depicting some disabled individuals as "work shy" or "faking" their disability. Nevertheless, it is arguably the case that within the advanced capitalist societies, a greater acceptance prevails, which tolerates disabled individuals receiving state support instead of entering the labor market. Grounded upon the dominance of the biomedical model, disabled individuals tend to have a special moral status, with their dependency largely accepted by the majority in society.

Considered disabled primarily through no fault of their own, individuals are viewed as having little, if any, control over his or her biological status. There is an assumption they would work if they could, but their bodies prevent them.[22] As a result they are generally thought of as entitled to support from welfare services.[23]

In this analysis, an essential role of the welfare state is reproduction. Individuals are "reproduced" in the sense of functioning as members of capitalist society, and as citizens who accept the class-based nature of this society. Chapter 6 discussed how social security plays an indispensable role in preparing individuals for the labor market who currently might not be working, as well as strictly reproducing their material conditions. Of all categories of individuals in society, those with disabilities are frequently subject to the welfare state's reproductive ambitions. In relation to disabled individuals thought deserving of social support, and accepted as not having to offer their labor power for sale, the welfare state assumes responsibility for reproducing their material conditions at a basic level. Defined as having limited value as a form of exploitable labor, many disabled individuals are recipients of welfare services that transfer a proportion of society's surplus to them to compensate for their exclusion from wage labor. As for social security recipients more generally, welfare provision for disabled individuals acts as a vital source of purchasing power that would otherwise largely be unavailable, allowing the disabled to obtain necessities that contribute to their reproduction. The purchasing power provided ensures an element of material and physical protection that will hopefully be accepted as a form of remuneration, quelling any opposition to capitalism and the conditions contributing to their inability to fully engage in the labor process. Additionally, socialized health services, despite potentially inflicting restrictive forms of intervention and control, often constitute significant methods of enhancing the physical existence for individuals.

Disability, Welfare, and the Reserve Army of Labor

Political scientist Deborah Stone, although not situating her analysis within a Marxist framework, illustrates the significance of the welfare state for establishing who is disabled. Disability, she asserts, is a socially constructed category allowing society to delineate the perimeter between ability to work and dependency, arguing welfare's purpose is to "keep everyone in the work-based distributive system except for the very neediest people, those who have legitimate reason for receiving social aid."[24] As an evaluative category, the state makes use of disability to determine the size of the labor force.[25] While recognizing this economic function, Stone primarily understands disability as a *"formal administrative category* that determines the rights and privileges of a large number of people."[26] Although important, this ignores the capitalist context within which the welfare state functions: that as a category disability identifies who is, and is not, capable of work.

Despite efforts to rate types of disability against clinical measurements, under capitalism disability is a fluid and not a fixed category. While the biomedical model may equate it with impairment, not all impairments are categorized as a disability. Value-laden judgments of medical professionals, activists, and the state influence whether an impairment will be given the status of a disability. Additionally, the welfare state determines who is considered disabled, with this evaluation not done in isolation from the mode of production. As already argued, defining disability is greatly determined by the corporeal requirements of the labor process. This provides the broad context within which evaluations are made and the basis upon which many social policies operate. The welfare system acts as the mechanism by which an evaluation is made as to whether someone is disabled based upon their ability to work. More specifically, who is considered disabled is bound up with the welfare state's role in regulating and reproducing the supply of labor. Who is identified as disabled will often vary depending upon the specific needs of capitalism at any historic moment, with the category of disability, and the organization and operation of disability policies, adapted to correspond with the historical socio-economic context, and the needs of the accumulation process.[27]

This flexibility is inextricably related to the role individuals with impairments have as part of the surplus labor population.

As stated in the previous chapter, this surplus population constitutes a disposable resource for capital, a pool of potential labor to be exploited when needed.[28] Specifically, it has the role of regulating the existing labor force that, "during periods of stagnation and average prosperity, weighs down the active labour-army; during the periods of over-production and paroxysm, it holds its pretensions in check."[29] For Marx, the reserve army of labor has the function of quelling discontent during periods of economic decline, and moderating exuberant challenges during times of prosperity, crucially with regard to wage demands.[30] Above all, it acts as a method of control, restraining wage growth and reducing labor costs.[31] As made clear above, Marx considered individuals with impairments as living in a state of pauperism, the bottom strata of the reserve army of labor. However, over the last half-century or more in the advanced capitalist nations, it is more accurate to depict disabled individuals as, overall, occupying a fluid position between groups who experience severe poverty outside of the labor market and the stagnant population who experience irregular employment.

Far from a static concept, the composition of the reserve army of labor is thus fluid, with the boundaries between it and the labor force penetrable. For example, the history of the advanced capitalist nations shows periods of both integration within, and exclusion of disabled individuals from, the labor market in response to historically specific conditions of accumulation.[32] Over the last decade in Britain, as in many other advanced capitalist nations, the focus has once again turned to working-age disabled people as a source of labor, exemplified by social security reforms designed to increase their participation within the labor force. Attempting to transform them to floating members of the reserve army of labor through a reassessment of their corporeal status, evaluated against the labor process, the welfare state has intervened to reconceptualize the category of disability.[33]

Welfare Reform and the Disabled Labor Force

During the course of the 2010s, welfare retrenchment had detrimental consequences for a significant number of individuals and social groups throughout Britain. However, among the hardship experienced by many, a valid argument is that those with disabilities were most severely affected. Of the proposed austerity measures in 2010, reductions to social security (excluding pensions) and local government services amounted to 50 percent of all desired savings. Social security benefits for disabled individuals and their carers amounted to 40 percent of the total expenditure upon non-pension benefits in Britain, while social care services, which are heavily used by the disabled, constituted 60 percent of all local government expenditure. As a result, targeting reductions in these two areas inevitably meant that disabled individuals and those who support them were hit nine times harder by welfare reductions than other citizens.[34]

Obscuring the boundaries between welfare and labor market policy, efforts were made in the 2010s to transform the disabled into floating members of the reserve army of labor through social security reforms. While continuing to provide an element of out-of-work income support, these reforms were utilized as an economic policy to bolster the provision of labor.[35]

In Britain, Employment Support Allowance (ESA) has come to constitute the primary income-replacement benefit for the working-age disabled. Initially introduced in 2008, it has established itself as the principal means whereby a disabled person's work capability is assessed, having emerged as a major disability policy.[36] Argued as a means to provide greater opportunities for individuals to obtain employment, ESA policy has expanded the supply of labor through a process of "upskilling." Integral to ESA have been efforts to define who is disabled, with this predicated upon a Work Capability Assessment (WCA) evaluating an individual's corporeality, and biological status, in relation to expected performance within the labor force. Subsequently, entrenched within ESA is the assessment of a worker's claim to disability against the nature of the labor process that contributes greatly to evaluating disability status.

Prior to the implementation of ESA, the main income-replacement benefit for working-age disabled individuals in Britain was Incapacity Benefit (IB), which also had a work-based assessment component. However, under the ESA this assessment process has become more stringent.[37] The threshold for defining disability has increased, meaning those who under past assessments may have been identified as disabled, and incapable of work, have a greater chance of being deemed suitable for employment. When reassessing individuals during the transition period from Incapacity Benefit to ESA, between 2010 and 2013, 22 percent of applicants who were previously entitled to support under the old program were considered capable of work after assessment by the new WCA criteria.[38] Central to ESA, therefore, has been redefining disability when assessed against the labor process, in an effort to construct a greater number of individuals as able-bodied.

While ESA is a mechanism to regulate who occupies the category of disability, overwhelmingly this is for the purpose of determining who is, and is not, thought suitable for wage labor. After the mandatory WCA, if deemed ineligible for support, applicants are identified as Fit For Work and compelled to join the ranks of the unemployed as able-bodied. If entitled to ESA, individuals can be sorted into two groups. The first is the Work-Related Activity Group. Accepted as disabled, they are nonetheless considered as having some capacity to work in the future. Subsequently, they are mandated to engage in work-related initiatives or risk losing their benefits, but do not have to obtain employment. Despite reduced expectations that individuals will actively pursue work, the out-of-work income support for this group is limited, and in 2017 it was reduced for new claimants, now comparable to unemployment benefits, in the hope this would encourage people to "voluntarily" opt into the labor market. Finally, if regarded as unfit for work, applicants are placed into the Support Group, with no expectation they engage in work or work-related activities. They receive a rate of benefit greater than those in the Work—Related Activity Group.

Of all completed WCAs between October 2008 and September 2018, 34.6 percent of applicants had been placed into the Support Group, followed by 40.3 percent deemed Fit For Work, and 25.1 percent categorized as part of the Work-Related Activity Group.[39] Subsequently, just under half of applicants were categorized as floating members of the reserve army of labor, either compelled to pursue work immediately or engage with work-related training, demonstrating they were interacting with the labor process. As a welfare policy, ESA has primarily contributed to the creation of a surplus labor population, comprising indivudals who are prepared for future work. Less concerned with identifying current employment opportunities, ESA's objective has been to expand the reserve army of labor with people who have the required skills and attitudes, and can seamlessly transition to the labor market when needed. That the supply of potential labor should grow at a rate greater than opportunities to enter the labor market is not an aberration, but fundamental to the success of the reserve army of labor. Wage restraint and social control is only feasible with an increasing supply of surplus labor existing outside of the labor market.[40]

Instrumental to identifying able-bodied members of the floating reserve army of labor (those classed as Fit For Work), ESA's role in maintaining and reproducing individuals still officially classed as disabled, but who have been identified as capable of joining the floating surplus labor population, is most succinctly demonstrated in relation to the Work-Related Activity Group. One of the primary purposes of the mandatory work-based initiatives is to ensure the long-term reproduction of their ability to labor. This component of ESA has the responsibility of ensuring that this particular group, although officially classified as disabled, retains their capacity to work while outside of the labor market. As floating members of the reserve army of labor, it is crucial that their ability to labor is reproduced, if not for the present then for the future should they be absorbed into the labor market after any mandatory reassessment of their ESA claim is made, and their status as disabled potentially reevaluated.

For the remaining applicants of ESA who are not required to seek work or engage in work-related activities, their corporeal nature is acknowledged as insufficient to correspond with the requirements of the mode of production, with little expectation they join the ranks of the labor force. Although, given the fluid nature of the disability category, this means in the future they may be assimilated into the labor force, or transferred to the Work-Related Activity Group category. As part of the Support Group, the state has a responsibility to maintain them. Their material existence is underpinned by the redistribution of a proportion of society's surplus produced by members of the labor force. While there are those in this category who have severe impairments and are unlikely to have the capacity to work regardless of the conditions of labor, there are also many within the Support Group who continue to remain victims of capitalism's exclusionary economic organization.

National League of the Blind and Welfare Reforms

The disability movement in Britain during the 2010s was a preeminent force of opposition against attacks upon the state's social security provision. As the previous chapter demonstrated, disabled individuals displayed fierce resistance, often taking direct action, having experienced significant threats to their previous welfare entitlements. As journalist and disability activist Ellen Clifford made clear, individuals in receipt of disability support, as well as those who rely upon the state to support them, such as family and friends who provide informal care to disabled relatives and friends, were significantly disadvantaged by reductions to social security provision during this decade.[41] Although at the heart of the class struggle against welfare cuts, a common perennial disadvantage has been, and remains, the challenge of coordinating collective action among activists due to divisions predicated upon a diversity of impairments among the disabled. The 2010s in Britain saw a disability movement

that reflected a unique strength of solidarity, as welfare retrenchment targeted all disabled groups. The strength of feeling of injustice,
and the levels of oppression, resulted in differences among disability
activists being put aside, allowing them to position themselves as
a united collective at the center of the wider anti-austerity movement.[42] Epitomizing the class struggle that engulfed the state, and
the ability of labor to utilize welfare provision within this struggle,
the disability movement fought tirelessly to reverse welfare reductions. That the state has been an object that the disability movement,
and working-class disabled individuals, have attempted to influence
and wrestle concessions from as part of the wider struggle against
capital, dates back over a century, as the example of the National
League of the Blind (NLB) exemplifies.

Collectively organizing to combat their oppression, and identifying the state as a means of support, the NLB came to prominence
in the years prior to the First World War. Grounded in the labor
movement, the NLB emerged as a trade union at the end of the
nineteenth century, officially affiliating with the Trade Union
Congress (TUC) in 1902, and the Labour Party seven years later.
Working in trades such as piano tuning, basket weaving, and rug
making for many blind members of the labor force exploitation
and oppression was severe—they were the victims of not just capital, but also having to work in degrading conditions for charities.
In response to this exploitation, the NLB was established in 1894.

As the twentieth century dawned the NLB, attempting to counteract their oppression, embraced the principle of state welfare as
an institution to support their role within the class struggle. For
historian Matthias Reiss, the NLB's effort to combat exploitation
was to agitate for "Parliament to pass a bill which provided direct
state aid for blind people outside of the framework of charity."[43]
For NLB, the state, not charity, should have responsibility for the
welfare of blind individuals. Specifically, state welfare support was
to be understood not paternalistically, but as an instrument of
liberation, with state resources and services depicted as means to
enhance their freedom. Anticipating the principles of the social

model of disability, the NLB viewed society, not blindness, as contributing to oppression and stifling their productiveness. The state was in a position to combat this, in particular alleviating blind people of their poverty and guaranteeing them the opportunity to work.[44] As early as 1898, the first general secretary of the NLB, Ben Purse, advocated state employment for blind members of the labor force, with this position evolving to include national and municipal workshops, a national wage, as well as a sufficient state pension. Many blind members of the population had been victims of the state's authoritarian and disciplinary nature during the nineteenth century, having experienced life under the Poor Law and the workhouses. Again, as with the actions of the disability movement during the 2010s, the state represented both an authoritarian institution, but also an institution that had the potential to offer support and protection against destitution and exploitation if it could be influenced by labor.

From its early years, the NLB developed a reputation for direct action, with this solidified once it became a member of the TUC, which garnered the support of other unions and socialists. In the years running up to the First World War, the NLB made its presence felt, organizing demonstrations and strikes. And though still cooperating with charities in an effort to improve conditions within this sector, state support remained its ultimate intention. By 1919, both the Labour Party and the TUC supported legislation that would provide visually impaired individuals with state assistance. After the Armistice, with the ranks of the NLB expanded by wounded ex-servicemen, the British government, already mindful of the potential possessed by demobilized servicemen to revolt, began to take the movement more seriously.

Throughout 1918 and 1919, demonstrations for the expansion of state welfare for visually impaired indivduals were organized by the NLB, with events culminating in 1920. Under banners reading "Justice not Charity" on Easter Sunday 1920, having secured support from the labor movement, a contingency of 171 members of the NLB from the north of England, Ireland, and South Wales set out on a hunger march to London to demand state legislation. They marched for twenty days, waiting a further five to meet with Prime Minister David Lloyd George, with growing public sympathy for their position, the demands of the NLB were too much for the government to withstand, and it had no choice but to implement the Blind Persons Act in September 1920. As part of the legislation, the age of pension entitlements for visually impaired individuals, in this first instance men, was reduced from 70 to 50 years old, while municipal governments were charged with the responsibility of providing work for visually impaired members of the labor force. Although not meeting all the demands of the NLB, the Blind Persons Act was historic. Illustrative of the collective efforts of disabled members of the labor force to organize and take action, this protest arose from their position as some of the most exploited members of the labor force. They identified state welfare as essential to enhancing their economic and social position, with their direct action understood as a vital weapon for labor within the wider class struggle.

Almost a century apart, the actions of both NLB and DPAC exemplify collective efforts by arguably the most vulnerable members of the labor movement to take direct action to resist exploitation and oppression, seizing upon the welfare state as integral to this. For DPAC, although having the long-term aims of a radical reorganization of society, the defense of existing welfare provision, as well as further reforms, were understood as crucial for both the immediate benefits of labor and the long-term transformation of society. Reductions to disability welfare benefits and health and social care services have dominated the era of austerity. Despite the valiant efforts of many campaigners, and the welcomed victories achieved, disabled individuals remain some of the hardest-hit victims of capital's efforts to curtail welfare expenditure. As Clifford correctly argues, the material conditions of disabled individuals continued to decline throughout the decade, while attempts to resist became ever harder as the resources many relied upon in the form of state support shrank. Yet what the decade demonstrated was a determination to resist the exploitation and oppression that pervaded the everyday lives of many, building upon a tradition stretching back to the NLB, as well as situating at the heart of this opposition a sense of justice and a fight for equality. The welfare state was integral to this.

Disability and Justice: An Alternative

Rather than a physiological issue, disability is a form of oppression and discrimination. While impairments have characterized people across space and time, and exist as a biological reality, disability is a capitalist construct, determined by the system's drive for accumulation, which conflicts with the corporeality of individuals with impairments. This oppression is reinforced by the state, managing and regulating their social status as either dependent or occupying various positions within the surplus labor population. With capitalism at the heart of their exclusion, disabled individuals are central to the class struggle.

More than two decades into the twenty-first century, in many advanced capitalist nations, including the United States and Britain, with the exception of examples such as DPAC, disability rights activism has been subsumed into the political mainstream, diluting its once radical nature.[45] In Britain, Michael Oliver and Colin Barnes addressed the "professionalization" of disability politics, noting a decline in the authority of grassroots organizations as large charities and governments adopted the causes advocated by the movement, sanitizing it goals.[46] Moreover, epitomizing the appropriation of the disability cause by the political mainstream, rather than focusing upon the structures of inequality, a "rights-based" approach has dominated the agenda, reflecting a liberal preference for equal opportunities. Undoubtedly, legal equality is essential, but as other oppressed groups can testify, it is not the solution. The emancipation of disabled individuals through the granting of equal rights has become an end in itself. But social justice will always be elusive if oppression is concluded to be primarily the result of largely volunteristic discriminatory practices and attitudes, rather than the consequence of an economy that has commodity production at its heart. As Russell asserts, "If we conceptualise disablement as a product of the exploitative economic structure of capitalist society . . . then it becomes clear that anti-discrimination legislation . . . is insufficient."[47]

As long as capitalism remains the dominant mode of production, the oppression of disabled people will continue. Under an alternative economic system, one democratically organized, where the purpose of labor is to be fulfilling, creative, and meaningful, it is quite conceivable, as disability advisor Roddy Slorach argues, that many individuals who find themselves currently excluded from the labor process due to impairments would have greater opportunities to participate.[48] A radical reorganization of the production process, allowing the full inclusion of individuals with impairments, is fundamental for their liberation. A democratically accountable economic system would accept and value varying abilities and skills, ensuring work for all.[49] In this situation, this is not work underpinned by profit, but by human need, allowing all members of society, whether having impairments or not, to achieve a sufficient material existence for themselves, and, crucially, to engage in the labor process in a way that affirms their humanity. For those with the most severe physical and cognitive impairments, some of society's most vulnerable members, the democratic reorganization of society and the economy is essential to guarantee a life free from poverty and marginalization. A democratically controlled welfare system, offering the support and material needs required by individuals unable to partake in the labor process, provides the opportunity to live a life of dignity and respect, rather than being measured against a scale of productivity.

8

Health

Fundamental to the Marxist method is dialectics, with change emerging from the interaction between objects and phenomena. The health status of any individual arises from the dialectical interaction between the materialism of their body and the materialism of the society that the body inhabits. The body has its own biological structural organization, governed by its own internal biological forces. Without doubt there exists an expected way in which the body functions, reflecting its inherent structural operation, which, when operating in the expected manner, contributes to the existence of good health. Yet both good and poor health, do not, in many incidences, simply arise from the positive and negative functioning of the body. Instead, as crucial as the biological operation of the body is, the structural organization and operation of society, with differing social environments, plays a vital role in influencing how someone experiences health.

Capitalism and Poor Health

Marx and Engels were acutely aware of the detrimental impact capitalism can have on the health of working people. Because of the material conditions of production, Marx stressed that "Every organ of sense is injured in an equal degree by artificial elevation of the temperature, by the dust-laden atmosphere, by the deafening noise, not to mention danger to life and limb among the thickly crowded machinery, which, with the regularity of the seasons, issues its list of the killed and wounded in the industrial battle."[1] Moreover, he made reference to the "victims of industry, whose number increases with the increase of dangerous machinery, of mines, chemical works,etc., the mutilated, the sickly."[2] As much as Marx understood how the fervent desire for increased accumulation negatively impacted the health of the labor force, it was Engels who provided the first detailed Marxist understanding of the relationship between capitalism and health.

Engels said that the root cause of poor health was capitalist production. The severe oppression and exploitation of the working-class had serious ramifications for the health of the labor force. The organization of capitalist society "placed the workers under conditions in which they can neither retain health nor live long." Additionally, "Society knows how injurious such conditions are to the health and life of the workers, and yet does nothing to improve these conditions."[3] The capitalist class were aware of the brutal impact production had on the health of the workers, but their failure to mitigate the poor conditions meant capitalism was committing social murder.[4]

Urban growth, Engels made clear, resulted in overcrowding and pollution, with serious health implications. Contributing to the development of respiratory complications was the burning of coal, a common source of heat in the meager dwellings of the working class, and consumed in abundance by industry. Consequently, air quality was severely compromised, filled with carbon dioxide, sulphur, and nitrous oxide, blackening the skies, buildings, and lungs of the individuals who had no choice but to work and reside in those surroundings. "The lungs of the inhabitants fail to receive the due supply of oxygen, and the consequence is mental and physical lassitude and low vitality."[5] Roaming the streets of Manchester, a city at the heart of the industrial revolution in Britain, Engels observed a working class who were "pale, lank, narrow-chested, hollowed-eyed ghosts," having "languid, flabby faces, incapable of the slightest energetic expression."[6]

In addition to working within polluted and dangerous conditions, the homes of many members of the labor force were severely injurious to health. Frequently, the experience of domestic life was one of overcrowding, with rooms that rarely received natural light and lacked sufficient ventilation. Furthermore, the working-class streets of industrial Britain were densely built, preventing an adequate supply of clean air, and the overwhelming majority did not have access to clean water and sanitation. As Engels posited in relation to this last point, "They are deprived of all means of cleanliness. . . . They are obliged to throw offal and garbage, all dirty water, often all disgusting drainage and excrement into the streets, being without other means of disposing of them; they are thus compelled to infect the region of their own dwellings."[7] The direct impact upon the health of the working class was the spread of infectious disease.

Marx and Engels explained the inextricable relationship between the spread of disease and capitalism. And in the early part of the twenty-first century capitalism remains a powerful determinant of health, with the diffusion of both good and poor health broadly following the distribution of wealth and authority. However, within the advanced capitalist nations, the premise that social conditions influence the development of poor health is frequently concealed by an all-encompassing belief that health is largely related to the biological functioning of a person's body, or because of an individual's behavior. In the face of this conclusion, as Howard Waitzkin, Alina Perez, and Matthew Anderson stress, there occurs a constant need to reassert to each generation the understanding that societal and material factors influence the etiological development of disease.[8] The economic and social organization and operation of capitalist society give rise to social and economic inequalities that constitute the root causes of many health issues, and exacerbate others. The essence of capitalism, such as its relations of production, the inherent drive for increasing accumulation, and the oppression and exploitation of workers, are the origins from which the unequal distribution of good health develop.

Corporeal Productivity

Good physical and mental health is a fundamental need and has figured prominently within the class struggle. In response, most of the advanced capitalist nations have established varying forms of universal state healthcare. To deny the benefits accrued to labor of a state healthcare system would deride genuine improvements experienced by many within the working-class. Yet it is unquestionably the case that state systems have bequeathed to capital many advantages, in particular their role in the maintenance and enhancement of people's capacity to work. Within the advanced capitalist nations, this constitutes a fundamental objective of any healthcare system.[9] For capitalism, and from the perspective of capital's drive to expand surplus value production, the principal intention of a healthcare system is to ensure that the labor force has a level of health that is functionally useful to be productive.

As was discussed in chapter 7 on disability, under capitalism not all labor power is considered of the same quality. Poor health is detrimental to productivity.[10] Intervention, therefore, is required to ensure that a minimum standard of physical and mental fitness is obtainable by all members of the labor force. Consequently, a universal standard against which an acceptable level of fitness is measured has evolved. In response the state has intervened in many advanced capitalist nations providing, or greatly subsidizing, the provision of healthcare, to ensure this standard is obtainable by the majority. With the state tasked with ensuring a universal standard of physical and mental fitness for labor, this means the costs of reproducing the health of the working class are socialized. A socialized system gives capital the advantage that the contributions of business owners are much less than if they were more directly responsible for the healthcare of employees.

While a universal standard of physical and mental fitness is essential, this standard is not fixed. Historically, as capitalism has evolved, old production processes have been replaced by new ones. During the last century the advanced capitalist nations witnessed the decline of heavy industry and manufacturing and their replacement with service sector occupations, including the growth of the sales effort (advertising), the state, and financial activities. As capitalism evolves, the expectations of labor, in terms of skills, behavior, aptitudes, abilities, and physicality have also evolved so that labor can adapt to the changing requirements of the production process. Astutely aware of the relationship between corporeal capacity and productivity, Marx recognized how a transformation in the productive process required a different type of corporeality. As capitalism became more technologically intense during the mid-nineteenth century, less muscle power was required as machinery demanded operators who were considered more dexterous. The result was growth in the employment of women and children. "In so far as machinery dispenses with muscular power," Marx claimed, "it becomes a means of employing labourers of slight muscular strength, and those whose bodily development is incomplete, but whose limbs are all the more supple."[11] Inferred from Marx's position is the understanding that differing methods of production require varying forms of physical attributes and abilities. Building upon this, as Vicente Navarro did, capitalism has matured and evolved with an increasingly complex division of labor with ever greater specialization in terms of corporeal abilities and skills. And, Navarro asserts, "This specialization demands great involvement and investment from the state in order to guarantee the reproduction of labor needed for the system."[12] In this process health systems are essential to helping equip members of the labor force with the desired levels of physical and mental fitness required to be productive, as well as corporeal fitness that corresponds with capitalism's specific historical productive needs.

The explicit use of state healthcare to promote productivity can be demonstrated in recent years by the English National Health Service's (NHS) overt incursion into supporting the employability of service users.[13] Establishing its long-term agenda, moving into the 2020s, it was asserted that "fast and convenient access to health services plays an important role in maintaining employment."[14] Arguing that mental health and musculoskeletal issues are prominent causes of labor force absences, service provision for such concerns needed to expand. Regarding mental health, the NHS has actively embraced the Individual Placement and Support (IPS) employment scheme, whereby, in partnership with the private sector, the purpose is to facilitate the transition to the labor market of individuals with severe mental health issues.

Healthcare as Ideology

Acting as a mechanism of social control, state health services embrace a particular understanding of health that is advantageous to the continuing dominance of capital. This is reflected in their organization, operation, and the knowledge base underpinning them.

Within the advanced capitalist nations, health is understood overwhelmingly as a biological phenomenon, which has significant ideological consequences. A capitalist conception of health is one that primarily perceives poor health as a state of physical incapacity causing suffering.[15] The result is that a reductionist position infuses the understanding of health under capitalism. Health assumes the status of an individual concept. Medical interventions are directed toward the individual, with the emphasis upon repairing the body to alleviate and prevent further health issues. Medicine under capitalism, Leonard Rodberg and Gelvin Stevenson correctly assert, "operates according to an individualistic, scientistic, machine model."[16] An individualistic approach to health has the consequence of diverting attention from the ways in which capitalism contributes to poor health and influences its distribution. A biologically deterministic understanding of health "deflects attention from multifactorial origin," Waitzkin contends, "especially causes of disease that derive from the environment, work processes, or social stress."[17] By masking the negative consequences of capitalism's organization and operation, the biological conception of health performs a vital ideological function. Individuals are viewed as sick, not society.[18]

Focusing on individuals rather than society has come to dominate state healthcare approaches to health prevention and intervention. The health promotion agenda of many healthcare systems coalesces around behavior, often employing the knowledge and methods of health psychology, to promote and reinforce the positive and negative consequences of various behaviors. Under capitalism prevention methods inordinately pivot upon behavior modification of individuals, rather than identifying the need for social and economic change. Behaviors such as drug and alcohol abuse, smoking, and unhealthy eating, among others, are identified as having negative consequences, but effort is placed upon changing individuals' behavior rather than considering the wider social and economic circumstances contributing to unhealthy outcomes. Additionally, although rarely explicitly stated, prevention has ingrained within it a victim-blaming approach, as often the person is characterized as at fault for his or her own poor health, having actively chosen to engage in unhealthy behaviors. Thus, the state has the responsibility to educate these people, and provide the resources to allow them to change their behavior. For capitalism, Navarro argues, this has the advantage of reinforcing "the basic ethical tenets of bourgeois individualism. . . . This life-style politics complements and is easily co-optable by the controllers of the system, and it leaves the economic and political structures of our society unchanged."[19]

In the Image of the Market: The English NHS

Up to this point the argument has been that state healthcare systems are advantageous for capitalism. First, through their role in reproducing labor power. Second, they have a vital ideological function, with their operation dominated by a biological explanation of health that emphasizes the individual and obscures the relationships between poor health, inequality, exploitation, and oppression. With increasing penetration over the last nearly four decades into many spheres of society, the relationship between capitalism and state healthcare is further exemplified in the way capitalism has attempted to shape state provision in its own image. Many state systems in the advanced capitalist nations, including those in Scandinavia, once a bastion of social democracy, have witnessed reforms of varying degrees of magnitude reflecting market values, in particular privatization. England has been at the forefront of this process, with successive governments since the 1980s forcing the NHS to operate upon principles such as choice and competition, and opening a lucrative market for global private healthcare operations.[20] While healthcare in England remains primarily publicly funded, its once universal nature as a state service has been especially challenged over the last decade, exemplified none more so by the introduction of the Health and Social Care Act (HSCA) in 2012, and subsequent legislation that followed.

In an attempt to model a state health system that reflects the values of the free market, the HSCA had to strike a blow at the heart of one of the fundamental principles upon which the NHS was established in 1948, that of universalism where all within society, regardless of social and economic division, are entitled to receive the same care and support. The HSCA abolished the NHS's foundational guarantee of universal care, instead requiring only "the Secretary of State . . . continue the promotion in England of a comprehensive health service."[21] While the onus remains on government to fund healthcare for individuals who live in England, responsibility of government to *provide* healthcare for all citizens was withdrawn. The provision of healthcare has been transferred to an autonomous public body, NHS England, controlling most health expenditure and directing the overall operation of the English NHS.

Prior to 2012, the administrative regional provision of the NHS was managed mainly by Primary Care Trusts (PCTs), which executed the government's health priorities. With the abrogation of the universal care requirement, however, this administrative system became obsolete.[22] PCTs were superseded by Clinical Commissioning Groups (CCGs). Composed of health professionals, including general practitioners as well as financial administrators, the CCGs' purpose was to secure the provision of services relating to secondary care, community health, and mental health and learning disabilities services. It is to these independent, quasi-private, consortia that much of the delivery of the English NHS devolved. The language of the HSCA allowed CCGs a broad margin of discretion regarding what services they provide: a group "may arrange for the provision of services or facilities as it considers appropriate" to "such extent as it considers necessary."[23] Freed from any legal mandate, the services and resources provided through NHS England now vary widely by clinic, city, and region. Further, in an act that strikes at the heart of the principle of universalism, the HSCA permitted CCG service providers to set their own eligibility and selection criteria for patients.[24] In July 2022, CCGs were abolished and replaced with Integrated Care Systems (ICS). Although an administrative reorganization, the fundamental principles underpinning ICS remain the same as those supporting the operation of CCGs. To limit the state's authority over the provision of healthcare, ICS lack any democratic control, but there exists the opportunity for the private sector to be represented on these boards.

Repealing government responsibility and delegating care provision to independent regional authorities has exposed the English NHS to an unprecedented threat of privatization. As part of the HSCA, the NHS was authorized to administer services directly or subcontract them to private providers. Although the circumstances for public provision remain, providers are legally compelled to outsource services. Couched in the language of "consumer choice" and patients' rights, the private sector must have an opportunity to provide services; any state monopoly over healthcare would be illegal. For this rapid privatization to occur, repealing the legal duty to provide universal care is required. Universal services allocate resources based upon need, whereas the private sector is always concerned above all with the pursuit of profit. The costs involved in delivery mean that some health services, communities, and patients are more profitable than others. Far from guaranteeing patients a fair "choice" of services and providers, private contractors are freed from any obligation to deliver services that might threaten their bottom line.

Working-Class Struggles for Healthcare

Having demonstrated some of the advantages state healthcare has for capitalism and how capital has attempted to shape the state's provision, it must be acknowledged that a system of state healthcare was historically central to working-class struggles in Britain. For many among the ranks of the working class, it was, and remains the case, abundantly clear how a state healthcare system is beneficial for protection against the worst excesses of the free market and exploitation.

Reflecting the argument made so far, at the start of the twentieth century the health of the labor force was an issue of great concern for British capital. Legislation allowed, for the first time in 1907, the provision of free health inspections in schools. In 1911, with the passing of the National Insurance Act, the state assumed responsibility for the provision of health insurance, through which at least the more affluent members of the working class would benefit. Except for broad public health legislation during the nineteenth century, both pieces of legislation exemplified the emerging acceptance by the state to directly intervene to help ensure the health of the population. The then Chancellor of the Exchequer, David Lloyd George, proclaimed, "Money which is spent on maintaining the health, the vigour, the efficiency of mind and body in our workers is the best investment in the market."[25]

Notwithstanding capital's concerns, the introduction of health reforms did not solely arise because of the need for enhanced productivity. Behind the introduction of health insurance was the working class. As Navarro observed, "The main reasons for that legislation were: first, the social demands by labour for increased wages, improved working conditions . . . and strengthened job protection and security."[26] Reflecting working-class concerns, the State Medical Service Association (SMSA) was prominent among radical voices campaigning for universal state healthcare. Public ownership of hospitals and health facilities, under the authority of municipalities, was essential for the SMSA, with all medical professionals becoming salaried employees of the state. Asserting the centrality of municipal government to aid access to healthcare, the position of the SMSA reflected that of the Second International, where it was maintained that municipalities were important sites of collectivism and socialist activity, with it being the responsibility of municipalities to ensure the collective provision of medical services and hospitals.[27] Stimulated particularly by the experience of the First World War, by 1918 the position of the SMSA was endorsed by a majority within the labor movement.[28] Even its more radical wing embraced the idea, with the Communist Party of Great Britain (CPGB) advocating for a free medical service in 1924.[29] By the end of the decade the CPGB had vehemently endorsed the establishment of a state medical service, free for all, under which most health services would be provided.

The successor to the SMSA, the Socialist Medical Association (SMA), established in the early 1930s, continued to commit itself to the municipal provision of healthcare. Affiliated with the Labour Party, the SMA was established upon the core principles of a state health system providing both curative and preventive services.[30] State healthcare was understood as having the potential to be essentially socialist in nature, offering equitable universal care provided upon collective principles. Exercising authority among labor's political organizations, the influence of the SMA was evident when the Labour Party obtained control of the largest English municipal authority, the London County Council (LCC), in 1934. Although constrained by the limited authority of municipal government, the actions of the Labour Party in London reflected the socialist value of state healthcare in practice where the objective of a "socialist programme for health in London" was pursued.[31]

Under the authority of the Labour Party the LCC championed the "municipalization" of London's hospitals, expanding the authority of the municipality over the hospital system. The result was that approximately 76 percent of all hospital capacity in London came under the jurisdiction of the local state.[32] Municipal ownership was considered integral to ensure hospital care was universally available. Moreover, further committing to the universal provision of healthcare, and in response to calls within the SMA to ensure that maternity provision was under public control, the decision was made guaranteeing that all women could expect a free ambulance service when they went into labor.[33] Although the limitations of municipal socialism within the context of capitalism was apparent, the influence of the SMA in London illustrated the potential of establishing a democratically controlled municipal health service, whereby provision traversed class boundaries and decision-making was devolved to the locality within which services were delivered.

The Second World War and a National Health Service

Securing the commitment of the British people to fight the Second World War could not rely upon calls to patriotism alone. Having endured the First World War followed by two decades in which many experienced poverty and unemployment, both capital and the governing elite recognized the need for pivotal social and economic reforms once the war was over, to avert what was felt to be a real threat to the social and economic order by the working class. Moreover, the war itself gave rise to a spirit of rebellion that was of deep concern for capital.[34] This desire for change manifested itself politically in the landslide election victory in 1945 of the Labour

Party. Although not as radical as the mood of the national labor movement underpinning it, this government introduced notable social reforms, including a national system of state healthcare in the form of the National Health Service (NHS).

That the NHS was imperfect once established is not in doubt. Its very existence owes much to a conservative medical profession, fearful of losing its independence, being offered financial concessions and being granted the ability to continue to operate privately as well as working for the state. Furthermore, rather than empowering municipalities with the delivery of healthcare and promoting democratic control, the NHS reflected socialist ideals and working-class values that endorsed central state ownership. But, while this might be so, this should not detract from the role and influence of labor in driving forwards its establishment, with it a significant working-class achievement.

If a single individual is associated with the establishment of the NHS, it is Aneurin Bevan, Welsh socialist and Minister for Health and Housing during the postwar Labour government. Steeped in the labor movement, having been a coal miner and trade unionist, he avowed, "A free health service is pure socialism and as such it is opposed to the hedonism of capitalist society."[35] The introduction of the NHS was without doubt a major victory for labor. It was the culmination of almost half a century of agitation for a socialized system of healthcare. In its original form the NHS went some way to reflect, as Bevan himself stated, a socialist system of healthcare as a service collectively provided, delivered by the state, and free at the point of use. Support for the principle of the NHS ranged from the Labour Party, the organized labor movement, to more radical elements such as the CPGB. Although a class compromise, its creation undoubtedly enhanced, as it continues to do, everyday life for most of the British population.

Opposing the Neoliberal Agenda

Moving forward to the present day, the NHS and its principles remain central to the lives of many working-class people in Britain. With nurses going on strike in the winter of 2022 and early 2023 for the first time since the creation of NHS, over pay and working conditions, a majority of the British public were in support, recognizing the value the service provides on an everyday basis and the need to defend it against underfunding.[36] Alongside the actions of nurses and doctors who unleashed a wave of strike actions across the NHS, efforts to defend the original principles of the NHS have been reflected over the last twenty years in the actions of Welsh governments. In contrast to its counterpart in England, the Welsh NHS has experienced a deliberate attempt to protect it from some of the worst excesses of neoliberal reforms, especially privatization.

Since political devolution to the nations of Britain, which saw the initial establishment of the National Assembly for Wales, and now the Welsh Senedd (Parliament), Wales has been continually governed by a more overtly left-wing Labour Party, in comparison to the character of its English counterpart, except for the brief period in which the Labour Party was under the leadership of Jeremy Corbyn. Responsibility for most core healthcare functions have devolved to Wales. As with NHS England, the Welsh NHS receives the great majority of its funding from the British Treasury. However, in opposition to the developments in England, the overall organization and planning of healthcare remains the direct duty of the Welsh government, which delegates responsibility to regional state organizations in the form of Local Health Boards (LHBs). In Wales there is very little market-driven distinction between purchaser and provider, as this was abolished in 2009, eradicating a previous system of fragmented competition. LHBs plan, design, and commission primary and secondary healthcare regionally, engaging with local government during the process. Therefore, the state is responsible for funding, planning, and delivering healthcare.[37]

The Welsh NHS has rejected the ideology of competition and the fragmented service it produces; instead, healthcare remains a planned system, directly achieved through mechanisms of the state. Privatization, rampant in England, is minimal in Wales. If anything, it has been rolled back: the years since the inception of the Senedd—its law-making powers first granted in 2006, and this authority enhanced further in 2011—have seen a continued reduction in the use of private facilities by the NHS, and little use of the controversial public finance initiative (PFI), whereby private consortia raise capital to finance the construction of healthcare facilities, which are then leased to the NHS at inflated prices until eventually becoming public property, often decades later.

Over the last two decades, Labour governments in Wales have been constrained by the limited autonomy afforded to the Senedd. Moreover, there are indeed examples of Wales pursuing welfare policies that reflect to a greater or lesser extent market ideals. But any accurate evaluation of the political and economic agenda over the last quarter of a century must recognize the greater preponderance of spaces in Wales free from market values. The continuing strength of public provision reflects not only a preference for planning over competition, but also a deeper ideological resistance to the neoliberal agenda that has now dominated English politics for more than three decades. The Labour Party in Wales has rejected this path, often invoking the proletarian national culture that shaped Bevan's worldview. Even as much of Wales's industrial base has disappeared, the Welsh Labour Party has framed its health policy agenda in Bevanite terms of solidarity, community, and universalism. Subsequently opposing developments in England, the last two decades in Wales have witnessed an explicit effort to defend the original socialist values that underpinned the establishment of the NHS and formulate them for the twenty-first century and the working class of the nation.

9

Housing

Aside from his observations in *The Condition of the Working Class in England*, Engels articulated the crisis of housing in his 1872 polemic *The Housing Question*. Rapid industrialization and urbanization had driven the German working class into overcrowded and unsanitary living conditions. Accompanied by an upsurge in the value of land, properties were demolished, including workers' accommodations, with the land used for more profitable purposes. The result was a desperate shortage of decent working-class housing. The idea that the housing shortage could be resolved by encouraging the workers to become property owners was ferociously dismissed as an attempt to integrate labor into the capitalist system. By conferring upon workers the status of property owners, capital was attempting to strip labor of its working-class character and bestow upon them the notion they are members of the property-owning classes. As Engels argued, "By an alteration of their proletarian status such as would be brought about by the acquisition of house property, the workers would also lose their proletarian character and become once again obedient toadies." Here, Engels was asserting the implicit ideological role the ownership of housing assumes.

Engels was eager to stress that the crisis could not be solved by increasing the quantity of housing; there were already plenty of houses if the existing supply was utilized appropriately. A solution to the housing shortage was rather "the expropriation of the present owners and by quartering in their houses the homeless and those workers excessively overcrowded." However, the state, unwilling to intervene and appropriate capital's property, would not implement any effective measures,. Recognizing the potential of the state if under the authority of the working class, Engels said that the solution was the abolition of capitalist social relations so that the working class could appropriate political power to ensure the collective ownership and provision of housing for all.

Marx: Housing and Accumulation

Although his analysis of housing as an issue was spasmodic, drawing upon the accounts of public health officials, Marx was profoundly aware of the state of working-class housing. At the heart of the housing crisis were the gross inequalities of wealth and opportunity in society. The inability of the working class to obtain good-quality housing was a consequence of their exploitation and housing's commodification and appropriation by capital.[1] Alongside capital's simple disinclination to invest within it, Marx proclaimed that the condition of working-class housing was intimately related to the spatial circulation of capital. "The more rapidly capital accumulates in an industrial or commercial town the more rapidly flows the stream of exploitable human material, the more miserable are the improvised dwellings of the labourers."[2] At the time of his writing, as is still the case today, capitalism exhibited an uneven geographical development, with the use of land and its value, as well as the availability of credit, determining the organization of the urban landscape. Over the last century the state had come to play a preeminent role in this process, with significant consequences for housing.

Frequently motivating the geographical concentration of capital is the existence of resources and services embedded in the local landscape that make investment in a location attractive. Geographer David Harvey writes that these resources can be understood as immovable fixed capital whose primary purpose is to assist in the creation of surplus value and profit. Such resources and services include office blocks and factory buildings, roads, shops, warehouses, airports, docks, power stations, sewerage systems, hospitals, and housing.[3] Much of the urban landscape is characterized by this form of fixed capital. Its impact, Harvey observes, is "for fixed capital embedded in the land—and this includes factories, offices, housing, hospitals, and schools as well as the capital embedded in transport and communications infrastructures—to act as a significant drag upon geographical transformations and the relocation of capitalist activity."[4]

With the expansion of capitalism, the mid- to late-nineteenth century witnessed a rapid development, and redevelopment, of many British towns and cities. Typifying this was the establishment of fixed capital assets supporting the concentration of capitalist enterprises and encouraging the establishment of new ones. In the process of establishing new forms of fixed capital the urban landscape was modified. When Marx was writing, a common consequence of this process was the demolition of working-class houses, moving many members of the labor force to even poorer residential dwellings. "Improvements," as Marx sardonically referred to them, "of towns, accompanying the increase of wealth, by demolition of badly built quarters, the erection of palaces for banks, warehouses, &c., the widening of streets for business traffic, for the carriages of luxury, and for the introduction of tramways, &c., drive away the poor into even worse and more crowded hiding places."[5]

For Marx, working-class housing was at the mercy of the commodification of the urban landscape. As capitalist activity expanded spatially, working-class housing was swept away and pushed further to the margins, displacing large swathes of the laboring population and forcing them to live in more confined and decaying conditions. As well as a physical process, this was as much an economic phenomenon. As capital usurped more territory, commodifying it, creating spaces that attracted greater flows of capital to profit from locational advantage, land rents increased, which not only impacted upon industry and commerce but also housing. Marx quoted a public health official in London in 1865: "Rents have become so heavy that few labouring men can afford more than one room."[6] Mirroring Marx's concept of differential rent, the advantages of location, such as the geographical proximity of services and resources, affected the value of land, which was reflected in the levels of rent paid by capital, as well as the rent paid by tenants. As economist Michael Berry clarified this phenomenon: "The more advantageously located the land, the larger the gain. The periodic payment . . . from land user to landowner represents a ground rent and when that payment rises, due to increasing locational advantage, it is capitalised into rising land prices."[7]

Although sporadic, the analyses of both Marx and Engels offer some basic principles upon which to establish an understanding of the relationship between housing and capitalism. Both identified the inability of the working class to access housing of a good standard because of housing's commodification, with working-class exploitation and oppression a fundamental barrier. Subsequently, as Engels was at pains to stress, it would only be with capitalism's abolition and the collective ownership of the means of production, and the working class taking political power, that the housing question would be solved. Yet Engels was aware of the potential barriers to the collective ownership and provision of housing. Not so much from the opposition displayed by capital, as great as this was, but as a result of the hegemonic influence of private property within society, potentially gripping the imagination of many among the workforce. In this sense, Engels identified the importance housing played ideologically, in that it helps to reproduce the relations of production by reinforcing the principle of private property.

Housing as a Commodity

As Marx and Engels made clear and as it remains today, housing is ultimately a commodity. Its production is overwhelmingly done under conditions of private production for profit. Given this, as a welfare service it is arguably the most complex for analysis. With little controversy, it can reasonably be claimed that historically in most capitalist nations there has been hesitancy to intervene and appropriate the responsibility for its provision. This is in sharp contrast to services such as health, education, and social security. From its construction to sale, housing involves the input of industrial, commercial, and finance capital. Most of housing's production and consumption is mandated by the dictates of the market, with exchange value determined by the value of labor, raw materials, and land. As with all commodities, its production is underpinned by the exploitation of the working class, and its consumption determined by the distribution of wealth and availability of finance. For sociologists David Madden and Peter Marcuse, housing in more recent years has entered a stage of hyper-commodification. Emerging as an instrumental source of wealth, all aspects of its legal and material inputs have become commodities from which profit can be generated. Subsequently, "the capacity of a building to function as a home becomes secondary," with wealth creation being of primary importance.[8] Because housing is primarily a commodity under capitalism, it has an ambiguous relationship with the welfare state, often having thrust upon it a marginalized status within the provision of welfare.[9]

Ideology of Housing

The continuing dominance of housing as a commodity and the reluctance by capitalist states to intervene in its provision has much to do with its symbolism and the ideological advantages it offers capitalism. As Engels made clear, the value of housing as a commodity, among other advantages, is that it reinforces the principle of private property and in doing so enacts a vital ideological tool. The ideal of its private ownership, and acceptance of the belief among many within the working class that ownership is obtainable, despite ever challenging financial obstacles to this in recent years, seductively draws many into accepting the principles and values of the free market. A tactic that was effectively used by the governments of Margaret Thatcher in Britain during the 1980s, where municipal housing tenants were given the opportunity to purchase their property from the municipal authority.

The importance of private property under capitalism is such that, Harvey asserts, it is "the beginning point and end point of all capitalist activity."[10] While private property exists in many guises, housing is commonly invoked to appeal to the mass of the population to persuade them of the moral righteousness and potential economic advantages of living under an economic system where private property prevails. Berry sees the potential of mass owner-occupation promoting the dissemination of values favorable to a system of private property among the working class.[11] Moreover, the appeal of homeownership is reinforced through the tantalizing possibility of increasing personal wealth through the appreciation of housing's value. Berry writes, "Owner-occupation encourages the spread of economistic orientations among workers."[12] Furthermore, owner-occupation can contribute to the fragmentation of the working class, as a form of tenure not all members are able to achieve since it is "usually open only to the more privileged strata of the working class, typically driving a wedge between skilled manual workers and white collar workers."[13]

Reinforcing the principle of private property is a key reason why the provision of housing has largely remained outside of the state. Health, education, and social security do not conform to an obvious private property form. They cannot be easily converted and utilized to illustrate the principle of private property. Housing, however, is a tangible commodity. As Harvey asserts, "To be private property . . . a thing or process has to be clearly bounded, nameable and identifiable. . . . . Not everything is susceptible to that condition."[14] Good health and education are largely intangible phenomena. Housing is readily identifiable as a form of private property given its clear material nature. Housing subsequently serves a crucial ideological function, symbolic of and promoting the notion of private property among the working class.

Reproduction and Contradiction

Alongside its function as a source of wealth and ideology, housing plays an essential role in reproducing the working class. Housing acts as the location and provides many of the conditions instrumental to replenishing an individual's ability to work, such as eating, sleeping, socializing, and relaxing. Moreover, it is a critical environment within which children, as future members of the labor force, are nurtured. Overall, it is a fundamental spatial location within which the family is provided with the elementary means to ensure its members acquire the skills and capacities to be productive. Households are essential to what historian Tithi Bhattacharya refers to as "people making" with "human lives under capitalism . . . brought into being and shaped within kinship units and community spaces."[15] The reproduction of the working class is crucial for the sustainability of capitalism. As Berry asserted, "It is clear that housing is a basic element in the reproduction of labour power at the level of sheer physical survival," as well as meeting the "functional requirements of a suitably skill-differentiated and increasingly productive workforce."[16]

Although housing is vital for the reproduction of capitalist social relations, a glaring contradiction exists. Housing constitutes a significant component of labor's reproduction, but the costs of this are not offered in full by capital in the form of wages. As essential as housing is for the reproduction of the working class, it is far from easily obtainable. Redistribution of income to the working class so as to ensure housing could be afforded immediately but is opposed by capital, as this would entail a significant transfer of wealth and power. Additionally, there is limited scope to reduce the value of housing given the costs of its production. Any attempt to do so would impact upon property values and capital investment.[17] Considering such circumstances, the state has increasingly intervened to support housing's private production and consumption. Market supplementation policies include, among others, subsidizing construction capital, providing fiscal relief, influencing the rate of interest, and providing state-backed mortgage guarantees. Nonetheless, despite these initiatives, it has historically been the case that many members of the working class struggle to obtain housing via the market, both in terms of purchasing or renting it. Even with the state intervening with subsidies, there has always been a significant proportion of the labor force unable to obtain secure accommodations. Given the barriers and challenges faced by large swathes of the working class, an essential component of the class struggle has been to argue for housing's collective provision.

Class Struggle and Collective Provision

Reflecting upon the United States up to the time of their writing in the mid-1960s, Paul Baran and Paul Sweezy asserted, "At no time in the history of capitalism have the low income groups provided a market for new housing. . . . And there is not the slightest prospect that public housing will take on serious proportions as long as political power remains concentrated in the hands of a moneyed oligarchy."[18] Housing's commodification, they said, encourages its construction for those who can afford it, while its collective provision is fiercely contested. In Britain, the clash between commodification and collective provision has over the last century been fundamental to the class struggle, with the working class instrumental in agitating for public housing. As sociologist Norman Ginsburg discussed, from the late nineteenth century into the twentieth, "Working-class housing conditions have been one of the most crucial material factors pushing forward the class struggle."[19] Dominating working-class struggles for housing has been agitation for the state to take a greater role in its funding and delivery. For over a century working-class solutions to the housing problem have been to identify the collective provision of housing with the state fundamental.

The Rise of Municipal Housing

For much of the twentieth century the most direct form of state intervention within the British housing market was council housing. Owned and constructed by municipal government, tenants rented their property. At its peak, the involvement of the British state far exceeded that of many other advanced capitalist nations. As with so much of the British welfare state, a significant aspect of the push for council housing lay in the growing assertiveness of the working class. As economist Caroline Beale wrote, "State intervention in housing in the early twentieth century was in part a response to the increasing strength of working-class militancy."[20] The influence of the working class within, and upon, municipal government grew as labor's involvement with the democratic process became more intense. For instance, emerging from the radicalization of its district's labor force, the municipality of West Ham, East London, witnessed an increasing representation of labor, which seized control of the authority in 1898. As part of its agenda, the direct financing and construction of housing was a central priority. Furthermore, significant pressure from labor upon municipalities emerged externally in the form of local trade councils, with housing becoming an issue elevated to national importance in the early twentieth century—four national trade council conferences on housing were established between 1902 and 1909.[21]

In the same year as the working class took power in West Ham, the Workmen's National Housing Council (WNHC) was formed, the importance of which cannot be overestimated. Emerging from the Social Democratic Federation, which had been advocating for municipal housing for over a decade as part of its agenda for social-ist transformation, the WNHC founders were openly Marxist.[22] The WNHC forcefully lobbied local and national government for state provision of housing.[23] The prolific efforts of the WNHC were immensely significant in influencing local government to accept a greater role in the provision of working class housing.[24] And thus it was as a consequence of working-class representation within local government, as well as the external pressures of labor, that the working-class played a vital role in laying the foundations of council housing. As Ginsburg makes clear, by the eve of the First World War "working-class pressure . . . had all but achieved subsi-dised council housing."[25]

Although the actions of the working-class were indispensable, the growth of council housing was not without support from capi-tal. As early as the mid-nineteenth century, working-class housing conditions had captured the attention of many within the middle class. While paternalist thinking invaded the consciousness of some, others feared the ill-health emanating from the slums. Disease failed to respect the geographical boundaries of wealth. Moreover, for capital, the physical condition of the labor force was of significant concern, given its perceived impact upon Britain's global economic dominance. Subsequently, the concerns of capital provided additional pressures for the state to act. Beginning with the earliest public health acts, working-class housing therefore became an issue that the state started to accept some responsibility for. Yet it remained the impact of the working class that hit hard-est, with its influence contributing to the 1890 and 1900 Housing of the Working Classes Acts, which sanctioned the authority of municipalities to demolish slums and raise financing for the con-struction of new housing.[26]

Rent Strikes

Despite the foundations of municipal housing being established by the turn of the twentieth century, few municipalities engaged in construction on any significant scale prior to the First World War. Primarily, this was because of limited finances and subsidies. In the two decades following the end of the war, this would change as over 1.1 million council homes would be built.[27] Again, much of this was in response to the actions of the working class. The continuing struggles of the working class for accessible housing in this era is illustrated no more clearly than by the Glasgow rent strike of 1915.

With the outbreak of war, workers flocked to Glasgow, a center of naval shipbuilding and the munitions industry. To capitalize on this influx, landlords conspired to raise rents by up to 25 percent.[28] In response, thousands of tenants organized to oppose any increases, refusing to pay rent and physically blocking bailiffs from entering properties. Many industrial workers in the city also acted in solidarity by striking, inspiring similar protests in other British cities. In Glasgow alone, by November 1915, over 20,000 people were on strike. Though the strike's initial aim was to defy rent increases—in which it succeeded, with state-imposed rent controls introduced—its subtext was the advancement of municipal housing in order to combat the exploitation of the workin class by landlords.[29] As two participants in the strike asserted, "It is imperative that the State should accept the principle that a proper standard of housing for the people is a national charge."[30]

With the Glasgow rent strike integral to the state's expansion of council housing, Sean Damer describes the event as having "established that workers would be housed by the state as a right. Working-class demands had been articulated to a level where the state *had* to intervene to accommodate them."[31] Consequently, the state's intervention in the years immediately following the First World War was without doubt a victory for the working class. Direct from the rent strikes of the war years, a wave of socialists were elected to Parliament.[32] Among them was John Wheatley, a passionate campaigner for working-class housing, appointed Minister for Health in the first, brief Labour government in 1924. His namesake achievement, the Wheatley Housing Act, has been described as the "first substantial measure of legislative social-ism."[33] The law increased central government subsidies, allowing for the construction of over half a million municipal homes during the following decade. The same year of the first Labour government saw the Communist Party of Great Britain (CPGB) advocate for the provision of state housing, proposing the "nationalisation of all building and housing property," along with the provision of "grants and credits to local authorities for the building of houses by direct labour."[34] And so, the growth of council housing throughout the 1920s, combined with support throughout the labor movement, firmly established the principle of municipal housing as integral to a growing, but still piecemeal, welfare system.

Collectivism's Golden Era and Demise

Under the austerity of the 1930s, the construction of council homes slowed. But this was about to change. Although social democratic in practice, the sweeping to power in 1945 of the Labour Party exhibited glimpses of a more socialist-inspired agenda. Along with the NHS the expansion of council housing exemplified this, even if only in principle. Given responsibility for the development of council housing, in addition to supporting the establishment of the NHS, was Aneurin Bevan. Only the state, Bevan firmly maintained, could guarantee the universal provision of housing: "I believe that one of the reasons why modern nations have not been able to solve their housing problems is that they have looked upon houses as commodities to be bought and sold and not as a social service to be provided." Arguing further: "A house is far too complex a product of modern society to be left to unplanned initiative. Therefore, it is essential that the State should take a hand in the provision of this modern necessity and do so by making housing a service. That can only be accomplished by reposing it in the custody of a public authority."[35]

Left to the market, Bevan was saying, the pattern to housing's allocation would always be determined by those who have the financial means to acquire it. Yet housing is a fundamental necessity that all individuals must have. For this reason, it could not remain a commodity under the authority of those whose primary intention was its construction for profit. Housing, Bevan proclaimed, must be a social service and an essential element of the welfare system. For this to be achieved, the state had to take the lead in its production. Inspired by Bevan's vision, municipal housing expanded rapidly. From the late 1940s through the early 1950s, municipal homes constituted more than three-quarters of all new properties built, outnumbering private-sector developments in absolute terms until 1958.[36] Much of the costs were socialized: building and slum clearance were conducted by municipal authorities and their employees, and rents reflected the socialized costs of production rather than market values.[37] For a few years immediately following the war, the British housing market came as close to public control as it ever has. This reflected a broad united front between a social democratic government and more radical elements of the wider labor movement, as exemplified by the CPGB who fully endorsed the state's provision of housing and slum clearance.[38]

In the years following, the construction of municipal housing continued, becoming an established feature of Britain's housing sector. For over two decades, the rate of new council homes built amounted to anywhere between 100,000 to 200,000 each year until the 1970s. By the end of that decade over 40 percent of the British population were estimated to be living in municipal homes.[39] Continuing to offer a source of secure housing for the working class, municipal housing's practical implementation was far from perfect. A lack of democracy, bureaucratic management by local government, and limited investment devalued its potential. Moreover, exemplifying the less than harmonious reality of municipal housing, the 1960s and 1970s witnessed sporadic revolts of collective action by tenants, particularly in the form of rent strikes initiated, to varying degrees of success, against municipal authorities raising rents. Despite this reality, the principle of municipal housing remained significant through the postwar era for the working class, continuing to be supported and valued in principle even if its execution and delivery generated friction. During the last two decades of the twentieth century, however, the idea of council housing and the ideal of the collective provision of housing was ferociously attacked, as housing became victim to mass privatization.

Reflecting the ideological role of housing, from the early 1980s a concerted effort was made to promote home ownership, to reinforce and accept the neoliberal principles of individualism and self-reliance. Key to this was forcing municipal authorities to offer to sell their housing to tenants. As one notable Conservative politician declared at the time, a key purpose of privatization was to promote "the attitudes of independence and self-reliance that are the bedrocks of a free society."[40] With approximately 40 percent of the population having the state as their landlord, this represented, for right-wing politicians and businesses, not only an unacceptable level of state involvement in the lives of individuals and a crowding out of the private sector, but also a very visible form of collectivism that challenged the idea of private property. And so, as a consequence, the outright privatization of an integral aspect of the British welfare system ensued. Large swathes of municipal housing, throughout the 1980s up until the early 2000s, were privatized. Either in the form of tenants purchasing homes, or homes that remained under municipal control being transferred to private nonprofit housing associations, which from the 1990s onward become the principal providers of new social housing, as they primarily remain in the early twenty-first century.

Resistance and the Way Forward

Along with the NHS, council housing was one of the most radical elements of the British welfare system. The construction of state-owned housing was greatly influenced by decades of working-class pressure and a symbolic challenge to the values of capitalism, openly exemplifying a collective means of providing housing.

Even if in practice it was less than perfect, it made clear that an alternative was possible. Yet privatization was an overwhelming reassertion of capital's dominance. At present the number of council homes in Britain pales in comparison to their peak, yet the ideal remains at the heart of current working-class pressures for housing. Over the course of the last two decades a new breed of housing action groups have been established to defend and promote working-class housing and support working-class residents. Issues pursued include enhancing the rights of private rental tenants, advocating rent controls, campaigning for greater finance for the maintenance of social housing, opposing privatization of remaining municipal housing, and the expansion of working-class homes, which includes council housing.

A prominent force in support of municipal housing, especially in the late 1990s and early 2000s, was Defend Council Housing (DCH). A coalition, consisting largely of tenants, trade unionists, and socialists, DCH emerged as a true grassroots working-class movement. Established to uphold public housing and promote values of collectivism and solidarity, DCH recognized the creation and expansion of municipal housing as a major working-class victory. It fought to protect existing municipal homes from privatization, promote collective provision of new housing, and campaigned for sustained public investment, as part of the wider drive for a comprehensive welfare state.[41] It was at the municipal level where DCH has had the most success. Local DCH chapters tapped into a spirit of collectivism among existing municipal housing tenants, effectively coordinating opposition campaigns wherever the threat of privatization to remaining municipal housing arose.

In addition to DCH, more recent years have witnessed the growth of the London-based Radical Housing Network. This is a coalition of groups concerned with varying housing needs such as homelessness, the rights of private rental tenants, ensuring investment is available for repairs, sustainable housing, and squatting. All members are united in their fight for housing justice. As part of their "People's Housing Charter," the unequal access to housing, it is asserted, has been significantly exacerbated by the privatization of municipal housing over the last four decades. For one member of this organization, Social Housing Action Group (SHAC), which represents tenants of social housing schemes and their employers, part of the solution to ensure a sufficient supply of working-class housing is the construction of at least one million council homes, as well as extending the rights of municipal authorities to purchase empty properties and convert them into council accommodation.[42] It is significant that the last two decades have witnessed a reverse in the decline of council housing, albeit a slow reversal. From a low of 130 new council homes completed in 2004–05, by 2021–22 this had risen to 4,080.[43] This is nowhere near enough to combat the crisis of working-class housing, and not the only solution, as cooperative housing offers much value to the working class. However, the increasing number of municipal homes built, and the centrality of this as an important solution for many housing groups, not only reflects the continuing importance of this ideal for working people but that working-class pressure has once again stimulated its expansion.

------- 10 -------

Education

Closing the second chapter of *The Communist Manifesto*, Marx and Engels identified the state as crucial for the transition to socialism—when in the hands of the working class the state has the potential to be an instrument of revolution. Public ownership of land, transport systems, communication infrastructure, the centralization of credit, as well as the extension of the state's authority over the means of production, was enthusiastically recommended. Concluding their exposition, Marx and Engels approvingly endorsed the public provision of universal education. "Free education for all children in public schools," they proclaimed.[1] A few years later, Engels made a similar point, writing, "Education of all children, from the moment they can leave their mother's care, in national establishments at national cost."[2]

Formal education, and its institutional and organizational provision, did not preoccupy the thoughts of Marx or Engels, but they nevertheless made scattered reference to it.[3] For Marx, the provision of mass education supported by the state was essential for the working class to assert itself. But, as integral as the state was, there were limits to the state's intervention. Marx scholars Brian Simon and Glenn Rikowski argue that though Marx accepted that the state should raise revenue for the funding of education, as well as regulating the curriculum and teachers as professionals, it should play little role in the delivery and control of education.[4] Making clear his position in the *Critique of the Gotha Programme*, and moving beyond what was endorsed in the *Communist Manifesto*, he proclaimed, "Elementary education by the state is altogether objectionable. Defining by a general law the expenditures on elementary schools, the qualifications of teaching staff, the branches of instruction, etc. . . . Government and church should rather be equally excluded from any influence on the school."[5] That is, the state should facilitate the provision of education, but it should not be the educator. As Simon contends, Marx's preferred position was one where the working class took control of the delivery of education through the establishment of locally elected school boards.[6]

Although not offering a specific program with respect to the content of education, Marx did embrace a holistic understanding of child development. Addressing the First International in 1866, he said that education should include mental instruction, physical education, and technological instruction (the latter point commonly referred to afterward as polytechnical education).[7] Education should enhance an individual's intellectual capabilities, physicality, and vocational skills. That education should be combined with labor was a characteristic of both Marx and Engels's understanding. Reflecting attitudes of the time, Marx considered it vital to integrate children into the labor process: "We consider the tendency of modern industry to make children and juvenile persons of both sexes co-operate in the great work of social production, as a progressive, sound and legitimate tendency."[8]

With reference to Robert Owen, whose actions provided an indication of what a socialist education system might look like, Marx asserted that education should "in the case of every child over a given age, combine productive labour with instruction and gymnastics, not only as one of the methods of adding to the efficiency of production, but as the only method of producing fully developed human beings."[9] Beyond these assertions, neither Marx

nor Engels offered much in the way of analyzing the relationship between capitalism and education. From within the classical
Marxist tradition, it was Lenin who insisted that capital would
utilize public education to ensure the working class had sufficient
technical skills to satisfy the needs of capitalism.[10] In a similar
vein, Bolshevik comrades of Lenin, Nikolai Bukharin and Evgenii
Preobrazhensky, writing two years after the Russian Revolution
of 1917, vehemently stated that schools under capitalism were
"adapted for the breaking-in of pupils to the capitalist system."[11]
While not granting the subject of education great attention, Lenin,
Bukharin, and Preobrazhensky touched upon a significant principle of any Marxist analysis of education. A crucial understanding
of education, and the education system, should explicitly illustrate
the fundamental relationship between capitalism and education,
and the extent to which education serves the needs of the economy.

Education as Commodity Production: The Reproduction of Labor Power

To appreciate the role of education in supporting economic growth,
educational institutions must be understood as integral to the reproduction of future and current labor power. For Louis Althusser,
"Available labour power must be 'competent' i.e. suitable to be set
to work."[12] Competency pertains to the working class having skill
levels considered productive. Schools supply students with necessary knowledge, both that which is general, such as literacy and
numeracy, as well as that which is relevant for more specific labor
market positions. Schools are sites of production in the sense that
students enter the education system as raw human capital and leave
as potential sources of profit and economic growth if equipped with
skills and aptitudes favorable to capitalism. The culmination of an
educational journey is, as sociologist Madan Sarup succinctly put it,
one whereby students are "transformed into products, commodities
to be sold on the market."[13] Fundamental to this process are edu-
cators, who are producers in the sense that they contribute to the

creation of the student as a commodity. The successful collective effort of teachers in this process is partially measured by a school's output in the form of examination results, which can subsequently confer upon the school a status reflecting the quality of the commodity produced. For a school, exam results are akin to corporation stock, reflecting value and performance.

School and the Reproduction of the Relations of Production

With the reproduction of the working class occupying a central position within any Marxist understanding of education, inextricably related to this is the centrality of education for reproducing the relations of production. This is instrumental in a Marxist analysis of education by economists Samuel Bowles and Herbert Gintis, *Schooling in Capitalist America*.[14] This book, one which achieved both acclaim and spawned a raft of critics, both Marxist and non-Marxist alike, remains a valuable approach to understanding education under capitalism today, and as a service of the welfare system.

Essential to the preservation of capitalism is the endurance of capitalism's class structure. But the reproduction of class relations is by no means inevitable. It requires methods and mechanisms to ensure this. For Bowles and Gintis, the education system plays a fundamental role within this process.[15] Although later criticized by Marxists and non-Marxists for being too deterministic, Bowles and Gintis argued succinctly that the education systems of the capitalist nations largely operate based upon the ordinances of the capitalist mode of production, reinforcing and promoting the social relations of exploitation and oppression. As they wrote: "Major aspects of educational organization replicate the relationships of dominance and subordinancy in the economic sphere."[16] More explicitly, these relationships are those "necessary to the security of capitalist profits and the stability of the capitalist division of labor."[17]

An elementary aspect of any attempt to reproduce capitalist social relations is the need to reproduce class consciousness.

This requires producing individuals who accept prevailing norms, values, and organizational structures conducive to the reproduction of capitalism and relations between capital and the working class. For Bowles and Gintis, schools facilitate the emergence of personality and character traits that correspond to the needs of the economy. "All major institutions in a 'stable' social system," they reasoned, "will direct personal development in a direction compatible with reproduction."[18] For the reproduction of capitalism, and the relations between capital and labor to prevail, the working class must possess certain characteristics that contribute to the continuation of capitalism. Compliance with and deference for authority, docility, acceptance of the work ethic, working for a reward, and an understanding of the world, Bowles and Gintis argue, are all vital character traits to be demonstrated by members of the labor force. Education systems are fundamental to this correspondence between the education system and the economic system: "The structure of social relations in education not only inures the student to the discipline of the work place, but develops the types of personal demeanor, modes of self-presentation, self-image, and social-class identifications which are the crucial ingredients of job adequacy."[19] In support, Sarup asserts that increasing levels of knowledge and technical expertise, as important as these are, do not dominate the preoccupations of employers. Instead, characteristics of adaptability and flexibility on the part of the labor force reign supreme as essential among employers, with schools instrumental to fostering these characteristics. "What employers are really anxious about are not standards of literacy and numeracy at all, but young people's *attitudes.*"[20]

That capital is especially concerned with the character traits of school-leavers (those who complete high school), graduates, and future members of the labor market was exemplified by research produced by the Confederation of British Industry (CBI), speaking on behalf of British capital. Attempting to define what employers understood by "work readiness," survey evidence in 2019 indicated that it was contingent on young people developing the right skills, knowledge, and character. Of these, character traits were understood as the most important quality, with employers requiring school-leavers and graduates to display appropriate behaviors and attitudes, followed by literacy and numeracy skills, previous work experience, and academic qualification. "Wider character, behaviours and attributes," the research stated, "are considered to be the most important consideration when recruiting school and college leavers."[21]

Culture and Ideology

As institutions where knowledge, attitudes, values, and behaviors are promoted, schools must be understood as ideological locations, promoting and suppressing ideas. As Bukharin and Preobrazhensky noted, soon after the Revolution, prior to the sweeping into power of the Bolsheviks, students were "imperceptibly stuffed with bourgeois ideology," and "infected with enthusiasm for all bourgeois virtues; they are inspired with esteem for wealth, renown, titles and order."[22] Consequently, schools are essential to facilitate ideologies that reproduce the relations of production.[23]

For Althusser, the ideological role of schools is such that he identified them as one of the primary ideological institutions within society. Second only to the family, schools are essential for the dissemination of manners and a respect for authority and hierarchy, which translate to expected behaviors and attitudes within work. Summing this up, Althusser asserted, "Reproduction of labour power requires not only a reproduction of its skills, but also . . . a reproduction of its submission to the rules of the established order, i.e. a reproduction of submission to the ruling ideology."[24] As educational theorist Michael Apple argues, schools act as powerful institutions within society for cultural reproduction. They are instrumental in defining certain ideas and perspectives as objective factual knowledge, but ultimately represent the interests of dominant classes.[25] The importance of schools in this process is that, like the family, they have children as a captive audience from their formative years. Children, who are legally obliged to attend schools are exposed to the ideas and values promoted by the school for much of the first two decades of their lives. The particular significance of education in this vein was recognized by Althusser: "It takes children from every class at infant-school age, and then for years, the years in which the child is most 'vulnerable' . . . it drums into them . . . methods, a certain amount of 'know-how' wrapped in the ruling ideology . . . or simply the ruling ideology in its pure state."[26]

As an ideological institution, the significance of schools resides in the implicit values and behaviors that are embedded in their routine structure and operation. Adopting a position similar to Bowles and Gintis, Rachel Sharp asserts that the ideological reproduction of capitalist social relations is entrenched in the practices of schools.[27] For instance, it can be reasonably questioned why there is an absence of detailed teaching of ideas that challenge capitalism, as well as no exposure to such phenomena as working-class perspectives in history and working-class literature. Instead, elitist perspectives on history are promoted, efforts to encourage students to embrace enterprise are made, nationalism is disguised as citizenship classes. Moreover, literature considered by elites as "classic" is endorsed, exemplifying an ideological infusion of knowledge that reflects an elitist and conservative middle-class perspective. What a curriculum includes and excludes has a significant ideological purpose, contributing to the maintenance of the capitalist social order. As Apple argues, "Social and economic control occurs in schools not merely in the forms of discipline schools have or in the dispositions they teach. . . . Control is exercised as well through the forms of meaning the school distributes. That is, the 'formal corpus of school knowledge' can become a form of social and economic control."[28]

Class Struggle and Resistance

The education system is vital for reproducing the working class and class relations, while establishing an ideological framework legitimizing the economic and social order, the pillars upon which a Marxist understanding of education rests. But, as significant as they are, caution must be taken not to lapse into simple determinism. Education services are situated within the context of class conflict. Rather than reduce their organization and operation to the needs of capitalism, the relationship between capital and the working class must be acknowledged as greatly influential. The education systems of the advanced capitalist nations must be understood as at the center of a dialectical process, shaped by the class struggle. A common but inaccurate criticism of Bowles and Gintis has been to interpret their analysis as deterministic where they are accused of arguing that the organization and content of education systems are determined by the needs of capitalism. As significant as this position is to their analysis, they recognize that education is significantly influenced by class struggle. Bowles and Gintis assert that the growth of mass education, as well as welfare more generally, was in large part a result of attempts to mitigate the consequences of the contradiction between capital and the working class.

For Bowles and Gintis, "The economic and educational systems possess fairly distinct and independent internal dynamics of reproduction and development. . . . The independent internal dynamics of the two systems present the ever-present possibility of a significant mismatch arising between economy and education."[29] Far from offering a superficial base and superstructure dynamic where the economy directly determines the superstructure, Bowles and Gintis recognize the broad autonomy of the education system. This independence allows for the education system to periodically develop in opposition to the needs of capitalism and capital, contributing to a disjuncture between education and the economy. In this situation, as Bowles and Gintis make clear, education becomes an "arena for struggle among social groups."[30] Stating their position more succinctly, they say: "Though the school system has effectively served the interests of profit and political stability, it has hardly been a finely tuned instrument of manipulation in the hands of socially dominant groups. Schools and colleges do indeed help to justify inequality, but they have also become arenas in which a highly politicized egalitarian consciousness has developed among some parents, teachers, and students." [31] With disjuncture between education and the economy laying the possibility for alternative educational approaches to emerge, Bowles and Gintis argue that more progressive elements within the ranks of capital have intervened to offer reforms to mitigate these challenges.

The degree of autonomy possessed by the education system not only allows for the development of politically conscious education professionals, but also, Bowles and Gintis assert, schools produce "misfits and rebels."[32] Despite the vital ideological role schools have, the contradictory nature of the education system under capitalism means that opposition and challenges to the school as an ideological institution is a potential reality. Schools, it must be emphasized, can give rise to and are sites of oppositional cultures. Subsequently, the working class must not always be understood as the apathetic victim of an education system operating for the benefit of capital.

Ultimately, capital is always at an advantage, able to define the nature and character of educational reforms and the nature of the educational system. Yet this should in no way detract from the role of class conflict in influencing the evolution of education and the influence of labor, which has forced reforms and concessions from capital. Although Bowles and Gintis's historic analysis pertained specifically to the United States, their assertion is applicable to many of the advanced capitalist nations when they state, "The impetus for educational reform and expansion was provided by the growing class consciousness and political militancy of working people." In response, capital has offered reforms to counteract working-class discontent and protect its own economic position.[33] Illustrative of the role of the class struggle, "The major actors with independent power in the educational arena were, and continue to be, labor and capital." Moreover, the structure of education "cannot be explained without reference to the demands of working people . . . and to the imperative of the capitalist class to construct an institution which would both enhance labor power of working people and help reproduce the conditions for its exploitation."[34]

Compulsory Education

Class struggle has permeated the evolution of the British education sector for well over a century. As the economy fell into relative decline during the late nineteenth century, a lack of education was identified as a vital contributory factor. As the Fabian Sydney Webb proclaimed, "It is in the classrooms . . . that the future battles of the Empire for commercial prosperity are being already lost."[35] For many bourgeois reformers education offered a direction from which British capital could potentially prosper, embracing the idea of compulsory state education of the working class to encourage economic growth. Yet while capital was making tentative steps to utilize state education to solidify the relations of production, by the latter decades of the nineteenth century the working class also began to champion the idea of education for their own cause.

Prior to the late nineteenth century, there existed a radical tradition among many within the working class for an independent system of education. Embraced by Chartists and devotees of Robert Owen, this tradition was deeply antagonistic toward institutionalized state education. It cultivated its own working-class pedagogy and passionately accepted that education must be political. Permeating its philosophical principles was that education should be "useful." Rather than an institutionalized experience, it was to be understood as related to practical activities with learning taking place in varying everyday situations, ranging from work to communal settings such as discussion groups, pubs, and trade unions.[36] Peaking by the mid-nineteenth century, as historian Richard Johnson makes clear, from the 1860s onwards this ideal of an alternative working-class system "was replaced by the demand for more equal access to facilities that were to be provided by the state . . . later socialists actually fuelled the growth of state schooling by their own agitations."[37]

By the 1880s working-class support was becoming apparent for municipally delivered, funded, and democratically controlled schools. As the position of the Marxist-inspired SDF made clear, "We hold that all education should be free for all and that everyone should be fully educated at the cost of the community." Moreover, for the Trades Union Congress (TUC), "The time has arrived for the government to establish a thorough system of national education," with "the public elementary schools . . . made free."[38] By the end of the century working-class pressure was too much to resist. Governments were forced to introduce grants subsidizing elementary education for all children. Further, with elementary schools under the authority of locally elected school boards, those on which labor was notably represented were instrumental in the complete abolition of school fees, as well as supporting the provision of free books and introducing provision for children with special educational needs.

The education system was identified by labor as crucial to ensure working-class children obtained other benefits. From the mid-1880s, the SDF campaigned vigorously for free school meals. This demand would also eventually include additional state interventions supporting the physical well-being of children, including school medical inspections. With these demands gaining traction among the wider labor movement, recognition grew that if children were to benefit from education, they must have optimal physical and mental health.[39] Poor health and the experience of hunger would constitute significant barriers to educational development if left unchecked. Although not an immediate victory, labor's pressure influenced the passing of legislation, introduced in Parliament by a Labour MP in 1906, that granted municipalities the authority, should they choose, to introduce free school meals. School medical inspections followed a year later.

Comprehensive Education: The Terrain of Class Struggle

The first decades of the twentieth century saw the working class continue to fight for compulsory state education. Focusing upon the secondary level, a concerted effort was made to pressure the government to expand the number of available places and abolish fees. Yet the pace of change was slow. As late as 1936, arguments against mandatory schooling beyond fourteen were made, with various voices in business asserting the value of children within the workplace.[40] It was not until after the Second World War that secondary education become universal and completely subsidized.

The labor movement wanted secondary schooling to assume the form of a comprehensive system of non-selective state education. Welcoming the expansion of state education after the war, the position of the Communist Party of Great Britain (CPGB) encapsulated the critical mood of the left in the postwar years, having demanded as early as 1924 for the public ownership of all schools, as well as universities.[41] Laying out its agenda, the CPGB strongly endorsed the abolition of private schools and proposed a unified non-selective secondary system of education under the control of national and local government. In their 1951 program *Britain's Road to Socialism*, it was asserted that under socialism "the present educational system, with its structure of class privilege barely modified by successive reforms, will be completely transformed into a single comprehensive system giving all children the best facilities and the fullest opportunities for development."[42] The predominance of teachers within the CPGB during the 1940s and 1950s contributed to comprehensive education gaining traction among both teachers' unions and the wider labor movement. Yet the reality until the 1960s was a divisive secondary system where a minority of children, at age eleven, would attend a grammar school should they be judged academic or, failing the entrance exam, attend a secondary modern school that directed children into more vocational and menial employment, and offered limited opportunity for them to continue their education beyond the age of 15. Although often offering advantages and opportunities to working-class children who did win a place in a grammar school, overall this system of secondary education continued to perpetuate inequality between working-class and middle-class children.

By the mid-1960s, support among the labor movement for comprehensive education was becoming hard to resist, this being secondary level education that is state-funded and under the authority of the municipal government. For radicals and the labor movement the value of comprehensive education was the principal ideal that they should educate children from all backgrounds ensuring that all are exposed to the same educational opportunities. Where authority allowed, various Labour Party–controlled municipal governments had already established the implementation of individual comprehensive schools in the years prior to the 1960s, in some cases, as early as the late 1940s. By 1965, a broad labor movement coalition of local Labour Party activists, Labour-controlled municipal governments, and individual campaigners, such as Brian Simon, who, as both an academic and member of the CPGB, was a vocal champion of the comprehensive system, forced the then Labour Government to order all municipal governments to establish a comprehensive system nationally and eradicate selective education. The then Secretary of State for Education, Anthony Crossland, although on the right of the Labour Party, accepted the role of comprehensive education in promoting the socialist ethic of both community and social cohesion.[43]

Without doubt, the left, ranging from its radical wing, as exemplified by the CPGB and organized labor, to local activists, played an important role in influencing the establishment of comprehensive education. Predicated on the values of all children having equal access to the same level of education, not only was it essential to promote educational equality but comprehensive education was accepted as vital to support social cohesion and solidarity. The comprehensive ideal, however, right from its earliest days was never implemented to its fullest and most radical potential. The setting and streaming of students based upon aptitude contributed to a continuing division among children often determined by their class rather than aptitude. The result was a half-hearted comprehensive education experiment. This lukewarm effort had little opportunity to become established before it came under attack from capital, which continues up to the present day.[44]

Market Reforms and a Neoliberal Assault

Since the 1980s there has been a gradual, sustained counteroffensive to the ideal of comprehensive education and its practical implementation. This has been underpinned by a free market agenda, attempting to establish an education system within which the values of choice and competition prevail. The extent to which this has influenced the organization of education, specifically in England, has been significant. Supported by governments of the right and left, market reforms have been justified on both ideological and pragmatic grounds. Characterizing these developments is what has been described as the creation of an education-business nexus. Schools have been shaped to operate like businesses, with business allowed to have access to schools.[45]

Introduced in 1981, the first prominent neoliberal incursion into the state system was the Assisted Places Scheme (APS). This allowed academically able children from poorer families to obtain a position at a private school, with the state subsidizing much of the cost. This single policy was an effort to promote market alternatives to state education, challenging the notion of a unified single state system, while supporting the fetishized principle of consumer choice. It was not, however, until the late 1980s and early 1990s that the neoliberal grip on education tightened. Reforms were introduced resulting in methods of financing schools that were in part predicated on having to compete for students. Grant-maintained schools were established, with autonomy from local democratic control and funded directly from central government to weaken the role of municipal government. Moreover, competitive tendering was forced upon all schools, with municipal governments legally obliged to evaluate whether the private sector could deliver auxiliary services for less than the municipal government itself. Exemplifying capital's attack in more recent years, one which has sparked overt resistance from the labor movement and many working-class parents, has been the establishment of academy schools.

Wholesale privatization of the education system is recognized as largely impractical, even if it remains an aspiration for those who venerate the principles of the market. Academies, however, come close to this ideal. Originally established in the early 2000s to take over "failing" comprehensive schools, academies are funded by central government with municipal government having no authority over them. In this sense they are considered independent, and they compete for pupils with existing comprehensive schools that remain under the authority of municipal government. Under the day-to-day stewardship of head teachers, the independence of academies allows greater control over the curriculum, teacher's pay and conditions (with teachers employed directly by the academy rather than municipal government), setting qualification levels required by teachers, whether a school specializes in a subject, and, to varying degrees, admissions policies.

Academies are sponsored institutions. Including among them private businesses, charities, faith groups, and parent-teachers associations, sponsors are responsible for establishing nonprofit academy trusts. These are responsible for the overall governance of the school, or schools; in 2019, there were 1,170 academy trusts that oversaw two or more schools, known as Multiple Academy Trusts (MATs). Emulating the governance of a corporation, trusts are composed of boards of directors that are responsible for the overall strategy, and a chief executive and team that operates the trust on a day-to-day basis. In 2022 over 80 percent of secondary schools in England were academies, or free schools that operate along similar principles. The growth in the number of academies over the last decade has been stimulated by an evolving government agenda. Initially, schools converted to academies if they were considered to be underperforming. In recent years, however, it has become a policy of successive Conservative governments that all schools should become academies. While prevented from making profits, they actively forge links with business in terms of encouraging work placement and providing training opportunities for students. Business can also have influence over the curriculum.

Labor has been vocal in its opposition to the academy movement. In 2022, Britain's largest teaching union, the National Education Union (NEU), openly criticized the drive to "academize" England's school system. There was no evidence, it was argued, that attainment levels of academies were better than in comprehensive schools. Indeed, data suggested the opposite, with an indication that high-performing municipally run schools can decline in their performance once they have been taken over by a trust. Moreover, teachers' working conditions were worse than those who work for municipally run schools.[46] This criticism came on the back of over a decade's working-class opposition in the form of strikes and protest. Although not coordinated on the national scale and having little success in reversing existing decisions, labor has nevertheless been victorious locally, blocking plans to convert existing municipally run schools into academies in the future. Moreover, outside of England, opposition to academies, and an adherence to the principle of comprehensive education, has characterized the policies of left-leaning devolved governments in Wales and Scotland. Both nations have retained an allegiance to municipally controlled comprehensive education, despite other market influences having infiltrated their education systems.

Support for comprehensive education by labor exemplifies the recognition of how important state education is for the working class. Capital, although not generally opposing the principle of state-funded education and its expansion, has nevertheless fought to influence and control its provision and operation. As recent years illustrate, capital will do what it takes to reduce the role of the state as provider of education and employer of professionals. But academies have also challenged the principle of equality of provision, even if the realities of the implementation of the comprehensive system resulted in a continuation of inequalities experienced by children in terms of outcomes. For labor the ideal of a true and radical comprehensive system remains powerful. A fully funded state comprehensive system, delivered by municipal government, is crucial for equality of access and opportunity for all children, but also essential for the democratic control of education.

—— 11 ——

A Radical Alternative for
a Progressive Future

Despite a tendency for some radical and progressive analysts to portray welfare as primarily beneficial to capital and a mechanism of oppression, the analysis in this book has argued that the situation is more complex. Although the welfare state has certainly been an implicit and integral component to the exploitation of the working class throughout the twentieth century, it is nevertheless the case that many of these welfare services have also been intrinsic to enhancing working-class living conditions. Throughout much of the last century, workers, we have seen, embraced many of the same welfare services to protect themselves as capital used to intensify exploitation of them. While taking place within the parameters and restrictions of a capitalist society, the welfare state has been a platform upon which the class struggle has been fought, and an instrument used by both capital and labor to assert their positions.

Welfare, subsequently, cannot be conceived as simply an instrument of oppression or exploitation. It has been, and remains, a genuine productive gain for labor. As history illustrates, the working class has been instrumental in influencing its organization and development, as well as defending it when under threat. For Lenin, "The essential thing for 'every real people's revolution' is the *smashing*, the *destruction* of the 'ready-made state machinery.'"[1] Over the course of the last century, Lenin's assertion gripped the imagination of many Marxists, becoming integral to an influential version of the Marxist understanding of the state. However, the value of this assertion for the working class is questionable. This is especially so today, with the state having evolved to perform many vital functions, including welfare, which Lenin saw only in its infant stages.

At the start of the twenty-first century, the "smashing of the state," if it meant the destruction in Britain of the NHS, social security, and what remains of municipal housing, would dismantle provisions the working class had established as part of the class struggle. As imperfect as these and other welfare services have been, and continue to be, in Britain and in other advanced capitalist nations, they have offered unquestionable means of support in times of need to counteract exploitation and support living standards. It can in no way be said that welfare has ever offered a vision of a socialist or anti-capitalist utopia. But it has gone some way to challenge the dominance of capitalism. Welfare services reflect, albeit in a limited fashion, collective and solidaristic values, and are largely available based on need, not the ability to pay. They have facilitated a greater opportunity to access and receive resources not dependent on an individual's market position.

Of sure benefit to the working class under capitalism, the same will be the case, though to an even greater extent, in a non-capitalist society where the working class have authority over society. Welfare will be an instrumental component of a new progressive society, one where the values of equality and social justice prevail. In this society, care and love for one another will dominate, in contrast to the suspicion and hate that frequently tear through the societies of the advanced capitalist nations. Under capitalism the dominant values of individualism, competition, and greed erect barriers between society's members. Yet, in a progressive society where care will characterize the interactions between all, collectivism, solidarity, altruism, and mutual support will reign. Such values will assist in the development of a cohesive society and the establishment of genuine communities within which all will feel integrated and accepted.

An anti-capitalist society will be a true "welfare society." Care and support for all will be paramount. For this to be successful welfare institutions will be more visible and prominent than they currently are. Rather than a society orientated to economic growth, the growth of human fulfillment will be the primary purpose. A progressive society will be concerned with the cultivation of human potential and everyone having the opportunity to achieve the best they can in terms of their physical, emotional, intellectual, and social capacities. Contentment, satisfaction, and happiness will be the overwhelming aspirations.

To conclude this analysis, I will outline how welfare provision may look in a society underpinned by values of equality, care, collectivism, altruism, and community. In this society welfare services will occupy a central position. They will be an institutional and organizational manifestation of care. Symbolically reflecting this will be a welfare society concerned with supporting and looking after all its members. Additionally, welfare will be integral to both reflecting and promoting essential core values of a progressive society. Ensuring that the working class are collectively in control of their own welfare, services in a progressive society will be both democratic and participatory, allowing for all individuals to be empowered as well as having the opportunity to participate in the collective care and support of one another. When this is so, the organization of progressive welfare services will need to evolve beyond what has been their nature in many advanced capitalist nations over the last century.

Care and the Community

For those of us who crave an alternative society inspired by justice, equality, democracy, and freedom, our fundamental concern must be a respect for humanity. We must desire for all the opportunity to experience contentment, fulfillment, and an opportunity to become the best we can. For this to be achieved, care and compassion must thrive. As revolutionary Marxist Che Guevara asserted, "The true revolutionary is guided by great feelings of love."[2] Our love for each other must determine the actions of activists and radicals and be the basis upon which a progressive society is organized, expressed in the actions of all members of society and institutions. Under capitalism there is an antagonistic relationship between expressions of love and compassion, on the one hand, and the values and operational needs of capitalism on the other. Values such as competition, individualism, and avarice prevail under capitalism. The dominance of these values erects barriers between people, creating atomized members of society who view one another as obstacles to their own progress and development. The consequence is a society of competition, selfishness, and conflict over resources and opportunities. Opportunities to experience fulfillment, love, and care are greatly reduced and unequally distributed.

Capitalism alienates us, from both ourselves as well as each other. Oppression and exploitation significantly corrupt the experience of being human, dulled and masked by capitalism's tyrannical operation. For neoliberal capitalism the ideal individual is one who possesses an entrepreneurial spirit and is guided by the values of self-reliance, self-improvement, and individual resilience.[3] This individual rarely expresses concern for others. Those around him or her are viewed as a resource to enhance their own, often financial and materialistic development. In this sense the neoliberal individual understands other members of society in terms of how they can make use of them for their own gain. Celebration of the individual, and the objectification of other members of society as resources, severely diminishes bonds of solidarity, collectivism, and altruism. But those values are essential for expressions of love and care to be made. Acting upon the basis of compassion, kindness, and benevolence toward all, as activists we must desire to break capitalist barriers of individualism, greed, and competition, and instead erect a system that promotes care and solidarity. For this to be the case, it is essential that the ideal of community becomes a reality, both in terms of all of us perceiving we are part of one, but also that the social infrastructure allows for communities to develop.

Community, Marxist sociologist Erik Olin Wright wrote, refers to those acts of support that occur during everyday life. As an idea, community expresses "the principle that people ought to cooperate with each other . . . from a real commitment to the well-being of others and a sense of moral obligation that it is right to do so."[4] As a phenomenon, the concept of community encapsulates the principle of solidarity and is underpinned by expressions of care between those who are members of that community. It is a social phenomenon within which all members display a commitment to support the growth and prosperity of one another. The importance of community, however, is not only so that care and compassion are expressed. It is from within the community that all individuals have the opportunity for the full development of their humanity. As Che Guevara said, "Opportunities for self-expression and making oneself felt in the social organism are infinitely greater." And further, "The individual will reach total consciousness as a social being, which is equivalent to the full realization as a human creature."[5] It is within a community where experiences of the mutualistic, cooperative and supportive nature of it prevail that allow every member of society the greatest opportunity to develop their emotional, social, and intellectual capacities to their fullest potential.

An anti-capitalist society must have community at its heart. It must be a society that opposes all values of capitalism and supports the common bonds of humanity. For this to become a reality, society must have institutions and organizations that simultaneously promote progressive values and principles and whose operations are underpinned by them. These institutions must encourage working people and all members of the community to behave in ways that reflect and reinforce these values.

Institutionalizing Progressive Values

For care and compassion to prosper, and for communities to develop, there must exist an appropriate social infrastructure that allows for the expression of these values. This requires the establishment of revolutionary organizations. Within a progressive society welfare will be crucial for the institutionalization of progressive values and to support the growth of communities. Radical welfare institutions will support the satisfaction of communal needs, such as health, housing, education, and income support, among others, but doing so in a manner that is progressive and anti-capitalist. Moreover, they will be essential to promote social solidarity and care among members of the community

Through the way welfare services would be organized and operate, welfare recipients and providers will be encouraged to act in a cooperative and altruistic manner allowing for the development of a progressive consciousness and to allow for expressions of care toward each other. It was the socialist welfare theorist Richard Titmuss who said, "Socialist social policies are, in my view, totally different in their purposes, philosophy and attitudes . . . from Conservative social policies. They are (or should be) preeminently about equality, freedom and social integration."[6] Arguing the importance of welfare for the promotion of equality, Titmuss's additional aspiration was that any progressive welfare system would also encourage the growth of social solidarity.[7] If we desire a new set of social relations, a progressive welfare system will be crucial for encouraging all working people to act based on mutual concern and care for others. This can be achieved by the way welfare services are organized and operate.

From the Old New Seeds Are Sown

Of the cooperative movement during the nineteenth century, Marx was adamant that it represented "within the old form the first sprouts of the new, although they naturally reproduce . . .

all the shortcomings of the prevailing system."[8] He was arguing that new organizations and social relations that opposed capitalist values could develop from within capitalism itself, although they would inevitably experience challenges shaking off capitalism's imprint. Articulating a similar point was the anarcho-syndicalist-influenced Industrial Workers of the World (IWW). In the 1905 preamble to their constitution, they made clear efforts to collectively organize under capitalism, and each struggle opposing exploitation exemplified the establishment of a "new society within the shell of the old."[9] Despite what might appear to be significant barriers and overwhelming odds against radical social change, it already has foundations within capitalism. This principle has been embraced by a current generation of radical activists such as Mason Herson-Hord, Aron Vansintjan, Jason Geils, and Katie Horvath, who enthusiastically argue, "If we want real change, should we draw up a sketch of a just society and then simply march toward it? We think it's better to look around and find the seeds of a better future—perhaps dormant—in the present, and nurture them into a viable alternative that can challenge and transform the world around us."[10]

Influenced by both historical and current working-class struggles, present-day capitalism already contains examples of organizations and institutions that can be utilized to aid the transition to an equal society, and from which a progressive welfare system can be carved. As Michael Lebowitz asserted at the beginning of this book, rather than a system containing institutions reflecting only the needs of capitalism, capitalist society consists of institutions that are also in opposition to capitalism. These are institutions and practices that already epitomize an alternative progressive system, representing foundations upon which a more equal and democratic economic and social life can be organized.[11]

For those of us who want an alternative system, who feel the injustices of capitalism, and who clamor for a socially just world free of exploitation, poverty, oppression, inequality, and division, it is important that we do not assume all that exists under capitalism is nothing more than exploitative and reflective of capitalist values. It is essential to recognize that the present-day advanced capitalist nation already possesses institutions and methods that have the potential to challenge capitalism. While many of these institutions need radical modification to do this, they nonetheless offer the possibility.

Of those existing institutions essential to support the development of a progressive welfare system, the state will continue to play an important role in the provision of welfare. While under capitalism state services can be punitive, state provision has broadly gone some way to represent a space operating outside of the market, exemplifying a rudimentary example of a collectivist approach to the provision and funding of welfare services. As such, a progressive welfare system must retain the positive aspects of what already exists, including a role for the state, although this must be radically reorganized to operate in a fully democratized and decentralized manner. However, in an anti-capitalist society, not only would the state retain an important role in the delivery of welfare, its actions will nonetheless be dictated by the authority of collective community-based organizations.

State welfare services have dominated the landscape of welfare provision in the advanced capitalist nations for over a century. But if a working class welfare system is to develop, and the values of equality, collectivism, democracy, and participation are to prevail, we must look beyond the state, even that ideal of a state legitimately under the authority of labor. Imperative to establishing a society underpinned by democracy and equality is to ensure the working-class have as much control over their lives as possible. For this to be a reality, all welfare services must be under the collective authority of labor and delivered as close to the working class as possible. This means welfare services must operate from within, and be delivered by, the communities where working people live and work. Although the local state will remain important to the provision of welfare in a progressive society, any manner of democratic modification to it will not bring it directly into the communities it is meant to serve. Subsequently, a shift in authority and power is required, with the collective institutions of the working class themselves ascending to dominance and the local state subservient to them. Many advanced capitalist nations already have a network of grassroots and community-based institutions, free of both the state and the private sector. In a progressive society these institutions will be integral to developing and supporting an anti-capitalist welfare system, which will be reflective of a partnership between a decentralized state system and community organizations, but with the community the dominant partner.

Resistance and Justice: The Case for Mutual Aid

So far it has been asserted that the creation of a progressive, and equal, society requires the promotion of a new set of values, ones that allow working people to experience care and compassion as well as allowing them to freely express such sentiments to others. This radical transformation of society's cultural base is inextricably tied to a renewal of society's material base, such as its institutions and organizations. For this, progressive welfare services are essential. With existing community-based institutions vital to establishing a progressive welfare system, society's renewal must allow the working class to rely less upon the state in a paternalistic manner and instead develop their own network and system of community welfare institutions. Aiming to move beyond the state and embrace institutions democratically controlled by members of society, this echoes the position of anarcho-communist Peter Kropotkin. Economic and political liberation, he proclaimed, "will have to create new forms for its expansion in life, instead of those established by the State," which will have to be "more decentralised, and nearer to . . . self-government than representative government can ever be."[12]

Kropotkin wrote these words over a century ago, and in the time since many of these new forms and alternative methods of organization have been established, although eclipsed by the state and largely organized in a fragmentary and basic manner. Of these institutions essential to establishing an anti-capitalist welfare system, specifically important are those that operate based on mutual aid and inclusive participation. The nature and specific organizational character of these institutions has varied historically. In the early part of the twenty-first century, they include cooperatives, friendly societies, community benefit societies, community land trusts, worker-owned business, and neighborhood assemblies.

With mutual aid a viable alternative underpinning the delivery of welfare, we must be clear as to what is meant by it. Mutual aid pivots on the free and voluntary association of individuals who collectively support the provision of resources for an identified common need. This association supports the development of an awareness of solidarity among those involved as participants, who recognize the shared needs of others. In many cases, those involved in the collective provision of a service are additionally recipients of the same service. In this sense, providers are also users, collectively facilitating the fulfillment of the needs of others and themselves. For mutual aid organizations to be emancipatory, rather than solely a means of resource provision, they must support participants to assert themselves in demanding their rights, their dignity, and encourage them to develop an awareness of social justice. Mutual aid organizations must operate as consciousness-raising institutions, exemplifying to participants and recipients alike the exploitative, authoritarian, and anti-democratic power structures of capitalism and the associated unequal distribution of resources and opportunities.[13] Mutual aid organizations have the purpose of supporting the material conditions of individuals, educating them, and supporting the development of a progressive consciousness.

Mutual aid offers an oppositional alternative to capitalism. Institutions underpinned by altruism, collectivism, inclusivity, and democracy are characteristically different than capitalist institutions, which are built upon, and reinforce, individualism, selfishness, competition, and suspicion of others. Mutual aid ensures a valuable institutional means of organizing individuals to oppose capitalism and agitate for progressive change. These institutions have great value as a form of protest under capitalism, and they symbolize an alternative organizing method. While having been overshadowed by state welfare it is nonetheless the case that their importance and potential have been reflected within the sphere of welfare for well over a century or more.

For much of the period between the mid-nineteenth and early twentieth centuries, mutual aid organizations predominated as systems of social support for the poor and working class in many advanced capitalist nations, as the foundations of the welfare state were being laid. For example, many working-class communities in Britain, often conceived as the birthplace of the cooperative movement during the nineteenth century, were characterized by a local structure of community-based mutual aid networks, both formal, in the sense of being intertwined with the organized labor movement, as well as organizations established on an informal basis. All, however, arose from the collective efforts of the working class. Out of necessity it was common for working-class communities to erect a system of mutual aid organizations to provide resources to collectively protect workers, on an individual basis, but also for the community as whole, against the uncertainties and insecurities of the free market. Working-class efforts to collectively support each other included, among other social issues, building societies to support the construction of working-class housing, medical aid societies, coffin clubs, friendly societies, and clothing clubs.[14]

The revolutionary potential of the working class through the creation of mutual aid and cooperative organizations has been exemplified in more recent years in Venezuela. Beginning in the 1980s, in response to the corruption and violence of the state, communities and neighborhoods forged the establishment of a network of local assemblies to debate local economic and social issues, but also with the intention to initiate the wider revolutionary transformation of the corrupt centralized capitalist state. Morphing into communal councils as local units of democratic control under the presidency of Hugo Chávez during the late 1990s and early 2000s, this initiative was strongly encouraged as part of Chávez's desire for a twenty-first-century socialism. To strengthen the influence of the councils and their efforts to promote socialist values, communes were established and enacted into law in 2010. Bringing together geographically neighboring councils, communes were created as an overarching democratically elected body representing each associated council. Described by political theorist George Ciccariello-Maher as spaces of socialism, communes obtained the authority to directly control economic resources to meet local needs. The purpose of each commune was to devolve democracy as locally as possible, resulting in the creation of cooperatively sustainable communities that could collectively meet their own needs.[15]

Over the last decade or more, austerity and welfare retrenchment in many capitalist nations have resulted in the growth of mutual aid societies as alternatives to support and organize care within a context of the state withdrawing its engagement.[16] As a method of providing welfare, mutual aid societies constitute an anti-authoritarian system, which is in stark contrast to the history of state welfare provision, demonstrating a valuable means of promoting solidarity among welfare providers and recipients. While many mutual aid societies have grown in response to the state abandoning individuals and communities, they should in no way be considered as only a means of plugging a gap left by the state. Rather, they offer a credible alternative that must be built upon and embraced to establish solid foundations for a progressive welfare system and socially just society.

Because of its collective principle and the subsequent pooling and sharing of inputs and outputs, mutual aid has always offered an opportunity for individuals to access resources and services unobtainable if pursued by individuals alone. In this sense, these organizations have been, as they will continue to be, vital for redistribution of resources, opportunities, and the pursuit of equality. As such, they are crucial to promote individual freedom. By allowing for the redistribution of and access to resources, mutual aid has the potential to ensure that individuals have an opportunity to be free from the challenges and barriers that arise from a lack of access to resources as healthcare, education, or income. An individual with poor health, limited education, or low income can in no way be considered free, given the barriers these present. Mutual aid offers all members of the community the opportunity of fair and equal access to welfare services, which will help promote their liberty. As Emma Goldman asserted, individual freedom is strengthened by cooperation: "Only mutual aid and voluntary cooperation can create the basis for a free individual."[17] It is for both the materialistic and cultural advantages offered that mutual aid has historically been embraced by progressives, and why it should continue to be identified as essential for the fight to transform society in the future and to establish a working-class welfare system.

The Municipal State

Mutual aid will act as the fundamental organizing principle underpinning a progressive welfare system, delivered by community-based cooperative institutions. Welfare must be under the command of service users and the communities within which they are located. All members of the community should have an equal opportunity to be democratically engaged in their delivery. To advance the values of collectivism, solidarity, and cooperation, welfare services will be structured to allow all members of the community to act in a manner that encourages mutual support. To accomplish this requires a radical reorganization of welfare services, with rejection of the current case under capitalism where many services are under the authority and control of a bureaucratic centralized capitalist state. A progressive reorganization of the welfare system would require a significant withdrawal of the state from their delivery. But it would not mean that the state takes no role at all. The state will remain significant in the form of a democratically controlled municipal state.

Transformation of society will be difficult, but the foundations of a progressive welfare state are already in existence in many capitalist countries. Conversely, the task is to expand upon and radicalize what already exists, fighting to establish new radical schemes, and educating members of society about cooperative and mutual aid organization. Establishment of a progressive society will be a process, not an event, consisting of stages. The use of existing community-based cooperative institutions could feasibly occur in the early stages, under the authority of politically conscious members of the community. They will attempt to engage with other members of the community through these institutions to raise political consciousness. Reorganization of the municipal state, however, will be more complex and likely to be achieved later in the transition phase after a sustained period of education and consciousness raising have encouraged many working people to pursue a radical democratic agenda. An initial effort to transform the local state and lay the foundations for change could come with election of progressive members of the community to positions within the municipal state, where the state could work in partnership with mutual aid and cooperative organizations.

The principal purpose of the municipal state will be to support the funding of radical welfare services. Cooperatives will have an opportunity to raise their own funds via various means. All organizations will be encouraged to join a federation of local and regional providers of a service, such as a federation of housing cooperatives, or the equivalent representing health cooperatives. Finance will be raised through the contributions of each cooperative to their respective federation, which will then be redistributed, when required, to each cooperative and to support the establishment of new ones. Additionally, finance will come from solidarity funds wherein members of an individual cooperative contribute to a pool of finance to be distributed to those in need who are members. Moreover, some cooperatives may engage in ethical business practices. One such example being that of a housing cooperative that also owns the lease to community land upon which the cooperative business operates and pays rent. Yet, despite all this, the revenue-raising capacity of the state will remain essential as will its ability to redistribute funds.

As essential as the community provision and development of welfare services is, there exists the real threat of unequal geographical distribution and access. Inequality of resources among individuals, social groups, and communities should be greatly reduced in a progressive society in comparison to experiences under capitalism. But there still exists the possibility of some form of relative inequality arising among communities. A consequence of this could be an inequality of provision between communities. To avoid this, the state must be utilized to ensure finance is distributed proportionally, recognizing that needs may differ between communities. Contributing to the equal provision of resources and services, it is essential for a progressive welfare system to be underpinned by the ethic of universalism. Services that are universal support the redistribution of resources and opportunities, thus encouraging the growth of equality. Additionally, they are essential to achieving social integration. With all members of one community able to access the same welfare services, and all communities receiving the same welfare services, feelings of solidarity and collectivism will grow among members of each community, and society generally. The importance of universal welfare services was summarized by the socialist welfare theorist Richard Titmuss, who argued strenuously that universal services were essential for social integration and the creation of "one society."[18] Tearing down barriers of social division and discrimination, universal welfare unites all members of society, because of both their common participation within, and eligibility to receive, the same service. Regardless of wealth, class, age, gender, ethnicity, disabled or able-bodied, universal welfare services are vital to establishing a society of collective unity. "In all spheres of need," he claimed, "some structure of universalism . . . provides a general system of values and a sense of community."[19] The municipal state will be integral to pursuing these goals.

A final brief point concerns the relationship between the municipal state and cooperatives within the community. Although developing a partnership with community cooperative organizations, the municipal state will be responding to the welfare needs and agendas of communities as a subordinate partner. At the heart of the state's operation will be individual committees representing each welfare issue, such as a committee composed of representatives of housing cooperatives and housing federations located within the legislative jurisdiction of the municipal state. Similar committees will exist composed of those representing other welfare services. Located within each community, local assemblies or communes will democratically discuss and decide a policy agenda relating to each welfare issue. Decisions here will influence representatives and committees within each municipal authority who act in relation to each welfare issue. The democratic process will dictate the actions of municipal government, democratically determining policy and budgets reflecting the decisions taken within the community by each assembly and their representatives within the municipal authority. Decision-making will remain within the community, a bottom-up process, with community representatives of grassroots-based welfare organizations represented at the municipal level. In this sense, the community will dictate the actions of the state with the state under the control of working people.

Looking to the Future

In our fight for an alternative society, the role of welfare cannot be overstated. Under capitalism organized welfare has always occupied a contradictory position. Capitalism has historically benefited from welfare provision, largely in terms of supporting the development of productive workers who can be exploited. The welfare systems of many capitalist nations have often been characterized by a miserly and authoritarian nature, an indication that welfare has always been considered a potential threat to capitalism. Erik

Olin Wright correctly acknowledges the potential challenge welfare presents to capitalism, asserting that many welfare services, although part of a capitalist state, have historically offered spaces in opposition to capitalism, underpinned by and organized along the values of collectivism and universalism.[20] Moreover, the values and ideals of welfare itslf conflicts with capitalism, with the values of love, care, and support permeating the notion of welfare support. These values are in opposition to capitalist values of individualism, competition, and self-reliance. It is for this reason that welfare systems have been so tightly controlled under capitalism and why welfare will be such an integral feature of a progressive society. The values of welfare will embody, and reflect, those of an alternative society to capitalism, one which has at its heart equality, democracy, solidarity, and love.

Notes

Introduction

1. Karl Marx and Friedrich Engels, *The Communist Manifesto* (London: Penguin,1985), 79.
2. Frederick Engels, "F. Engels Preface to the Third Edition," in Karl Marx, *The Eighteenth Brumaire of Louis Bonaparte* (New York: International Publishers, 2008), 14.
3. Larry Elliot and Patrick Wintour, "Budget 2010: Pain Now, More Pain Later in Austerity Plan," *The Guardian*, June 22, 2010, https://www.the-guardian.com/uk/2010/jun/22/budget-2010-vat-austerity-plan.
4. Brian Groom, "CBI Urges Deep Cuts in Welfare Spending," *Financial Times*, June 10, 2010, https://www.ft.com/content/53af1ada-73f4-11df -87f5-00144feabdc0.
5. The convincing victory of the Conservative Party in the 2019 General Election had little to do with the Labour Party retaining its overtly left-wing agenda. Instead, it was more a result of Labour's failure to adopt a clear position on Brexit and, in particular, endorse it, three years after the referendum vote, despite many within its traditional voting base being in support of leaving the EU. This was compared to 2017 when the Labour Party was clearer in accepting the referendum result.
6. James O'Connor, *The Fiscal Crisis of the State* (London: St James Press, 1973); Ian Gough, *The Political Economy of the Welfare State* (London: Macmillan Press, 1979); Claus Offe, *Contradictions of the Welfare State* (Cambridge, MA: MIT Press, 1984).
7. Michael Lavalette and Gerry Mooney, *Class Struggle and Social Welfare* (London: Routledge, 2000), 4.

8. Gerry Mooney, "Class and Social Policy," in *Rethinking Social Policy*, ed. Gail Lewis, Sharon Gewirtz, John Clarke (London: Sage Publications, 2000), 165–68.
9. Michael Lebowitz, *Between Capitalism and Community* (New York: Monthly Review Press, 2020), 11.
10. Ibid., 73.
11. Rosa Luxemburg, *Eight-Hour Day at the Party Congress*, https://www.marxists.org/archive/luxemburg/1902/09/19.htm.
12. Rosa Luxemburg, *Reform or Revolution* (London: Militant Publications, 1986), 31.
13. Paul Le Blanc and Michael D. Yates, *A Freedom Budget for All Americans: Recapturing the Promise of the Civil Rights Movement for Economic and Social Justice Today* (New York: Monthly Review Press, 2013), 14–15.
14. For more recent efforts by both authors, see Henry Giroux, *America's Education Deficit and the War on Youth: Reform Beyond Electoral Politics* (New York: Monthly Review Press, 2013); Henry Giroux, *Neoliberalism's War on Higher Education* (Chicago: Haymarket Books, 2014); Howard Waitzkin, *Medicine and Public Health at the End of Empire* (Boulder, CO: Paradigm Publishers, 2011); Howard Waitzkin, *Health Care Under the Knife: Moving Beyond Capitalism for Our Health* (New York: Monthly Review Press, 2018).
15. The main exception to this, albeit two decades old now itself, is Michael Lavalette and Gerry Mooney, *Class Struggle and Social Welfare* (2000); and Iain Ferguson, Michael Lavalette, and Gerry Mooney, *Rethinking Welfare: A Critical Perspective* (London: Sage Publications, 2002).

1. Capitalism, the State, and Labor Reproduction

1. Cynthia Cockburn, *The Local State: Management of Cities and People* (London: Pluto Press, 1980), 51.
2. Ian Gough, *The Political Economy of the Welfare State* (Basingstoke: Macmillan, 1981), 39.
3. Bob Jessop, "Recent Theories of the Capitalist State," *Cambridge Journal of Economics* 1, no. 4 (1977): 353–72.
4. Bob Jessop, *The Capitalist State* (Oxford: Martin Robertson, 1982), 28.
5. Ralph Miliband, *Class War Conservatism and Other Essays* (London: Verso, 2015), 3.
6. Bob Jessop, *State Theory: Putting the Capitalist State in Its Place* (University Park: Pennsylvania State University Press, 1990), 25.
7. Ralph Miliband, *Marxism and Politics* (London: Merlin Press, 2004), 94.
8. Vicente Navarro, *Medicine under Capitalism* (London: Croom Helm, 1976), 198–199.

9. Ibid., 100.
10. Marx and Engels, *The Communist Manifesto*, 82.
11. Ralph Miliband, *The State in Capitalist Society: The Analysis of the Western System of Power* (London: Quartet Books, 1983),7.
12. V. I. Lenin, *Collected Works*, Volume 29 (Moscow: Progress Publishers, 1974), 478
13. V. I. Lenin, *Essential Works of Lenin* (New York: Dover Publications, 1987), 275–76.
14. Louis Althusser, *Lennin and Philosophy and Other Essays* (London: New Left Books, 1977), 131.
15. Paul Sweezy, *The Theory of Capitalist Development* (New York: Monthly Review Press, 1970), 242.
16. Ibid., 243.
17. Frederick Engels, *The Origin of the Family, Private Property, and the State* (New York: Pathfinder Press, 1976), 158.
18. Miliband, *Class War Conservatism and Other Essays*, 68.
19. Ibid., 67.
20. Miliband, *Marxism and Politics*, 57.
21. Cockburn, *The Local State: Management of Cities and People*, 42.
22. Philip Corrigan, Harvie Ramsey, Derek Sayer, "The State as a Relation of Production," in *Capitalism, State Formation, and Marxist Theory*, ed. Philip Corrigan (London: Quartet Books, 1980), 5.
23. Ibid., 1.
24. Engels, *The Origin of the Family, Private Property, and the State*, 159.
25. Ibid., 160.
26. Ibid., 164.
27. Ibid., 159.
28. Ibid., 160.
29. Miliband, *Class War Conservatism and Other Essays*, 9.
30. Engels, *The Origin of the Family, Private Property, and the State*, 160.
31. Paul Corrigan and Peter Leonard, *Social Work Practice Under Capitalism: A Marxist Approach* (Basingstoke: Macmillan, 1979), 94.
32. Sean Damer, "State, Class and Housing: Glasgow 1885–1919," in *Housing, Social Policy and the State*, ed. Joseph Melling (London: Croom Helm, 1980), 74.
33. Ibid., 74.
34. Jennifer Dale, "Class Struggle, Social Policy and State Structure: Central-Local Relations and Housing Policy, 1919–1939," in Melling, ed., *Housing, Social Policy and the State*, 197.
35. Steve Bolger, Paul Corrigan, Jan Docking, Nick Frost, *Towards Socialist Welfare Work* (London: Macmillan, 1981), 18.
36. Miliband, *Marxism and Politics*, 87.

37. Ibid., 91.
38. Sweezy, *The Theory of Capitalist Development*, 248.
39. Ibid., 248–49.
40. Damer, *State, Class and Housing: Glasgow 1885–1919*, 74.
41. Caroline Bedale, "Property Relations and Housing Policy: Oldham in the Late Nineteenth and Early Twentieth Centuries," in Melling, ed., *Housing, Social Policy and the State*, 39.
42. Corrigan and Leonard, *Social Work Practice under Capitalism: A Marxist Approach*, 94.
43. Michael Lebowitz, *Between Capitalism and Community* (New York: Monthly Review Press, 2020), 122.
44. Ibid., 124.
45. Ibid., 125.
46. Erik Olin Wright, *How to Be an Anticapitalist in the Twenty-First Century* (London: Verso, 2021), 98–99.
47. Ibid., 103.
48. Ibid., 104.
49. Karl Marx, *Capital*, Volume 1 (London: Lawrence and Wishart, 1977), 536.
50. Cockburn, *The Local State: Management of Cities and People*, 54.
51. David Matthews, "The Working-Class Struggle for Welfare in Britain," *Monthly Review* 69, no. 9 (February 2018): 42.
52. Cockburn, *The Local State: Management of Cities and People*, 55.

2. Marxism and Welfare

1. James O'Connor, *The Fiscal Crisis of the State* (New York: St. Martin's Press, 1973); Ian Gough, *The Political Economy of the Welfare State* (London, Macmillan, 1981); Norman Ginsburg, *Class, Capital and Social Policy* (London: Macmillan, 1979); Claus Offe, *Contradictions of the Welfare State* (Cambridge, MA: MIT Press, 1984).
2. Paul Corrigan and Peter Leonard, *Social Work Practice Under Capitalism: A Marxist Approach* (Basingstoke: Macmillan, 1979); Lesley Doyal, *The Political Economy of Health* (London: Pluto Press, 1985); Howard Waitzkin, *The Second Sickness* (New York: Free Press, 1983); Madan Sarup, *Marxism and Education* (London: Routledge and Kegan Paul, 1978); Eric Shragge, *Pensions Policy in Britain* (London: Routledge and Kegan Paul, 1984).
3. Chris Pierson, "Marxism and the Welfare State," in *Marxism and Social Science*, ed. Andrew Gamble, David Marsh, Tony Tant (Basingstoke: Macmillan, 1999), 175.
4. Kirk Mann, "The Making of a Claiming Class: The Neglect of Agency in Analyses of the Welfare State," *Critical Social Policy* 5, no. 15 (1985): 62–74.

5. Michael Lavalette and Gerry Mooney, "Introduction," in *Class Struggle and Social Welfare*, ed. Michael Lavalette and Gerry Mooney (London: Routledge, 2000), 4–5.
6. O'Connor, *The Fiscal Crisis of the State*, 6.
7. Ibid., 101.
8. Ibid., 124.
9. Gough, *The Political Economy of the Welfare State*, 45.
10. Ibid., 45–46.
11. Ibid., 46.
12. Ibid., 47.
13. Offe, *Contradictions of the Welfare State*, 122.
14. Ibid., 125.
15. Ibid.
16. Vicente Navarro, *Crisis, Health, and Medicine: A Social Critique* (New York: Tavistock Publications, 1986), 44.
17. Iain Ferguson, Michael Lavalette, Gerry Mooney, *Rethinking Welfare: A Critical Perspective* (London: Sage Publications, 2002), 28.
18. John Saville, "The Welfare State: An Historical Approach," *The New Reasoner* 3 (1957–58); John Saville, "The Origins of the Welfare State," in *Social Policy and Social Welfare*, ed. Martin Loney, David Boswell, John Clarke (Milton Keynes: Open University Press, 1983).
19. Saville, "The Origins of the Welfare State," 12–13.
20. Saville, "The Welfare State: An Historical Approach," 5-6.
21. Saville, "The Origins of the Welfare State," 11.
22. Saville, "The Welfare State: An Historical Approach," 6.
23. Ibid., 9.
24. Ibid., 10.
25. Dorothy Thompson, "Discussion: The Welfare State," *The New Reasoner* 4 (1958): 127–28.
26. Ibid., 128–29.
27. Ibid., 130.
28. Ibid.
29. Paul Corrigan, "The Welfare State as an Arena of Class Struggle," *Marxism Today* 21, no. 3 (1977).
30. Peter Leonard, "Restructuring the Welfare State," *Marxism Today* 23, no. 12 (1979).
31. Norman Ginsburg, *Class, Capital and Social Policy* (London: Macmillan, 1979), 2.
32. Ibid.
33. Ibid.
34. Steve Bolger, Paul Corrigan, Jan Docking, Nick Frost, *Towards Socialist Welfare Work* (London: Macmillan, 1981), 17-18.

35. Ibid., 21.
36. Ralph Miliband, *Class War Conservatism and Other Essays* (London: Verso, 2015), 72.
37. Ralph Miliband, *Marxism and Politics* (London: Merlin Press, 2004), 163–64.
38. Erik Olin Wright, *How to Be an Anticapitalist in the Twenty-First Century* (London: Verso, 2021), 46.
39. Miliband, *Marxism and Politics,* 166.
40. Ibid., 164.
41. Ibid., 167.
42. Karl Marx and Frederick Engels, *Address of the Central Committee to the Communist League, 1850,* https://www.marxists.org/archive/marx/works/1847/communist-league/1850-ad1.htm.
43. Karl Marx and Frederick Engels, *Address of the Central Committee to the Communist League, 1850,* https://www.marxists.org/archive/marx/works/1847/communist-league/1850-ad1.htm.
44. Rosa Luxemburg, *Reform or Revolution* (London: Militant Publications, 1986), 30.
45. Ibid., 31.
46. Karl Kautsky, *The Class Struggle* (Chicago: Charles H. Kerr & Company, 1910), 89.
47. Ibid., 93.
48. Miliband, *Marxism and Politics*, 42.
49. V. I. Lenin. "Draft and Explanation of a Programme for the Social-Democratic Party," in *Revolution, Democracy, Socialism: Selected Writings, Lenin,* ed. Paul LeBlanc (London: Pluto Press, 2008), 91.
50. Paul Le Blanc, *Unfinished Leninism: The Rise and Return of a Revolutionary Doctrine* (Chicago: Haymarket Books, 2014), 29.
51. V. I. Lenin, *Marxism and Reformism* (1913), Marxist Internet Archive, https://www.marxists.org/archive/lenin/works/1913/sep/12b.htm.
52. V. I. Lenin, "Left-Wing Communism: An Infantile Disorder," 314.
53. Mark E. Blum and William Smaldone, *Austro-Marxism: The Ideology of Unity, Changing the World: The Politics of Austro-Marxism* (Chicago: Haymarket Books, 2017), 6.
54. Otto Bauer, "Parliamentarianism," in *Austro-Marxism: The Ideology of Unity, Changing the World: The Politics of Austro-Marxism,* ed. Mark E. Blum and William Smaldone (Chicago: Haymarket Books, 2017), 41.
55. Otto Bauer, "Programme of the Social Democratic Workers Party of German Austria," in *Austro-Marxism*, 504–9.
56. Ewa Czerwinska-Schupp, *Otto Bauer (1881–1938): Thinker and Politician* (Boston: Brill, 2017), 176.

57. Helmut Gruber, *Red Vienna: Experiment in Working-Class Culture, 1919–1935* (New York: Oxford University Press, 1991), 45–80.
58. Miliband, *Divided Societies*, 69.
59. Ibid., 74.
60. Ibid., 59.
61. Michael D. Yates, *Can the Working Class Change the World?* (New York: Monthly Review Press, 2018), 109.
62. V. I. Lenin, "Marxism and Reformism," https://www.marxists.org/archive/lenin/works/1913/sep/12b.htm,

3. Marx and Engels on Social Policy
1. Karl Marx, *Inaugural Address of the International Working Men's Association* (1864), Marxist Internet Archive, https://www.marxists.org/archive/marx/works/1864/10/27.htm.
2. Ibid.
3. Eric Hobsbawm, *Industry and Empire* (London: Penguin, 1999), 34.
4. E. P. Thompson, *The Making of the English Working Class* (London: Penguin, 2018), 212.
5. Ibid., 212–13.
6. Ibid., 222.
7. Karl Marx, *Capital*, vol. 1 (London: Lawrence and Wishart, 1977), 223.
8. Ibid., 558.
9. Ibid., 252.
10. Ibid., 224.
11. Hobsbawm, *Industry and Empire*, 100.
12. Marx, *Capital*, vol. 1, 252.
13. Ibid., 252–53.
14. Ibid., 225.
15. Frederick Engels, *The Condition of the Working Class in England* (Oxford: Oxford University Press, 2009), 178.
16. Marx, *Capital*, vol. 1, 265.
17. Engels, *The Condition of the Working Class in England,* 184.
18. Frederick Engels, *The Ten Hours' Question* (1850). Marxist Internet Archive, https://www.marxistsfr.org/archive/marx/works/1850/02/tenhours.htm.
19. Marx, *Capital*, vol. 1, 271.
20. David Matthews, "The Working-Class Struggle for Welfare in Britain," *Monthly Review* 69, no. 9 (February 2018): 35.
21. Marx, *Capital*, vol. 1, 276.
22. Ibid., 279.
23. Ibid., 280.

24. Paul Sweezy, *The Theory of Capitalist Development* (New York: Monthly Review Press, 1970), 246.
25. Marx, *Inaugural Address of the International Working Men's Association* (1864).
26. Marx, *Capital*, vol. 1, 268.
27. Ralph Miliband, *Class War Conservatism and Other Essays* (London: Verso, 2015), 9–10. That the state is an apparatus that acts in the interests of capital was fundamental to the position of Marx and Engels. However, this does not mean that the state must always be under the direct authority and influence of capital. As Marx argued of the Bonapartism state in France, and Engels did of the Bismarckian state in Germany, the state can possess a degree of freedom from capital, and it can implement policies that may not overtly be in capital's short term interests, or they may be opposed by a fraction of capital.
28. Sweezy, *The Theory of Capitalist Development*, 65.
29. Hobsbawm, *Industry and Empire*, 102.
30. Ibid., 104.
31. Marx, *Capital*, vol. 1, 257.
32. Ibid., 253.
33. Ibid., 257.
34. Ibid.
35. Ibid., 229.
36. Sweezy, *The Theory of Capitalist Development*, 248.
37. Marx, *Capital*, vol. 1, 229.
38. Ibid., *Capital*, vol. 1, 257.
39. James O'Connor, *The Fiscal Crisis of the State* (New York: St. Martin's Press, 1973), 124–49.
40. Ian Gough, *The Political Economy of the Welfare State* (London: Macmillan, 1981), 44–47.
41. Karl Marx and Friedrich Engels, *The Communist Manifesto* (London: Penguin, 1985), 79.
42. Marx, *Capital*, vol. 1, 283.
43. John Saville, "The Origins of the Welfare State," in *Social Policy and Social Welfare*, ed. Martin Loney, David Boswell, and John Clarke (Milton Keynes: Open University Press, 1983), 11.
44. Dorothy Thompson, "Discussion: The Welfare State," *New Reasoner* 4 (1958): 126.
45. Mishra, *Society and Social Policy*, 84.
46. Sweezy, *The Theory of Capitalist Development*, 242–43.
47. Ibid., 248–49
48. Thompson, "Discussion: The Welfare State," 126.
49. Ralph Miliband, *Marxism and Politics* (London: Merlin Press, 2004), 57.

50. Saville, "The Origins of the Welfare State," 13.
51. Frederick Engels, *The Origin of the Family, Private Property, and the State* (New York: Pathfinder Press, 1976), 160.

4. Capital and Welfare Expansion

1. Chris Jones and Tony Novak, "The State and Social Policy," in *Capitalism, State Formation and Marxist Theory*, ed. Philip Corrigan (London: Quartet Books, 1980), 146.
2. Eric Hobsbawm, *Industry and Empire* (London: Penguin Books, 1999), 156.
3. Harry Magdoff, *The Age of Imperialism* (New York: Monthly Review Press, 1969), 34–36.
4. Ibid.
5. Ibid., 160.
6. Ibid., 169.
7. J. R. Hay, *The Origins of the Liberal Welfare Reforms 1906–1914* (London: Macmillan, 1977), 30.
8. Tony Novak, *Poverty and the State: An Historical Sociology* (Milton Keynes: Open University Press, 1988), 91.
9. Jones and Novak, "The State and Social Policy," 147–48.
10. Ibid., 147.
11. Novak, *Poverty and the State: An Historical Sociology,* 105.
12. Hobsbawm, *Industry and Empire,* 124.
13. Ibid., 127.
14. Bentley G. Gilbert, *The Evolution of National Insurance in Britain* (London: Michael Joseph, 1966), 61.
15. Ibid., 70.
16. Ibid., 72.
17. Sidney Webb, *Twentieth-Century Politics: A Policy of National Efficiency* (London: Fabian Society, 1906), 9.
18. Chris Jones and Tony Novak, *Poverty, Welfare and the Disciplinary State* (London: Routledge, 1999), 129.
19. Jones and Novak, "The State and Social Policy," 150.
20. Gilbert, *The Evolution of National Insurance in Britain,* 77.
21. William Beveridge, *Unemployment: A Problem of Industry* (London: Longmans Green, 1909), 217.
22. Gilbert, *The Evolution of National Insurance in Britain,* 87.
23. Ibid., 90–91.
24. Gareth Stedman Jones, *Outcast London: A Study in the Relationship between Classes in Victorian Society* (London: Penguin, 1984), 334.
25. Hay, *The Origins of the Liberal Welfare Reforms 1906–1914,* 54–55.
26. Quintin Hogg, *Hansard: Social Insurance and Allied Services*, February

17, 1943, https://api.parliament.uk/historic-hansard/commons/1943/feb/17/social-insurance-and-allied-services.

27. Jones, *Outcast London*, 281.
28. Novak, *Poverty and the State: An Historical Sociology,* 70.
29. Ibid., 72.
30. Ibid., 73.
31. Karl Marx, *Capital*, vol. 1 (London: Lawrence and Wishart, 1977), 592.
32. John Charlton, *Class Struggle and the Origins of State Welfare Reform* (London: Routledge, 2000), 69.
33. Jones, *Outcast London*, 291.
34. Ibid., 285.
35. Hay, *The Origins of the Liberal Welfare Reforms 1906–1914,* 34.
36. Winston Churchill, *Liberalism and the Social Problem* (London: Hodder and Stoughton, 1909), 363.
37. Novak, *Poverty and the State: An Historical Sociology,* 85–86.
38. Engels, *The Condition of the Working Class in England,* 325.
39. Jones, *Outcast London,* 301.
40. Novak, *Poverty and the State: An Historical Sociology,* 122.
41. Pat Thane, *The Evolution of the British Welfare State* (Basingstoke: Palgrave Macmillan, 2009), 194.
42. Gilbert, *The Evolution of National Insurance in Britain,* 257.
43. Thane, *The Evolution of the British Welfare State,* 167.
44. Novak, *Poverty and the State: An Historical Sociology,* 137.
45. Jose Harris, *Unemployment and Politics: A Study in English Social Policy 1886–1914* (Oxford: Oxford University Press, 1972), 365.
46. John Charlton, "Class Struggle and the Origins of Welfare Reform," in *Class Struggle and Social Welfare,* ed. Michael Lavalette and Gerry Mooney (London: Routledge, 2000).

5. The Struggle for Welfare

1. Henry Pelling, *Popular Politics and Society in Late Victorian Britain* (London: Macmillan, 1968), 2.
2. James E. Cronin and Peter Weiler, "Working-Class Interests and the Politics of Social Democratic Reform in Britain, 1900–1940," *International Labour and Working-Class History* 40 (1991): 48.
3. Pat Thane, "The Working Class and State 'Welfare' in Britain, 1880–1914," *Historical Journal* 27, no. 4 (1984): 879.
4. Cronin and Weiler, "Working-Class Interests and the Politics of Social Democratic Reform in Britain, 1900–1940," 50.
5. Ibid., 49.
6. Chris Jones and Tony Novak, "Class Struggle, Self-Help and Popular

Welfare," in *Class Struggle and Social Welfare*, ed. Michael Lavalette and Gerry Monney (London: Routledge, 2000), 35–37.

7. Ibid., 37.
8. Thane, "The Working Class and State 'Welfare' in Britain, 1880-1914," 878–79.
9. Ibid., 881.
10. William Morris, *How I Became a Socialist* (London: Verso, 2021), 108.
11. William Morris, *Socialism and Politics*, https://www.marxists.org/archive/morris/works/1885/commonweal/07-answer.htm.
12. William Morris, *Communism*, https://www.marxists.org/archive/morris/works/1893/commune.htm.
13. Frederick Engels, *Letter to August Bebel*, 30 August 1883, https://www.marxists.org/archive/marx/works/1883/letters/83_08_30.htm.
14. Frederick Engels, letter to Friedrich Adolph Sorge, 10 November 1894, https://www.marxists.org/archive/marx/works/1894/letters/94_11_10.htm.
15. Social Democratic Federation, *Socialism Made Plain* (London: Modern Press, 1883).
16. Frederick Engels, *Daily Chronicle Interviews Engels*, end of June 1893, https://www.marxists.org/archive/marx/bio/media/engels/93 _07.htm.
17. Thane, "The Working Class and State 'Welfare' in Britain, 1880–1914, 882."
18. Graham Johnson, "'Making Reform the Instrument of Revolution': British Social Democracy, 1881–1911," *Historical Journal* 43, no. 4 (2000) 988–89.
19. Social Democratic Federation, *Socialism Made Plain*, 5–6.
20. Henry Hyndman, *Laborism, Impossibilism and Socialism* (1903), https://www.marxists.org/archive/hyndman/1903/05/impossibilism.htm.
21. Ibid.
22. Henry Hyndman, *State Socialists and Social-Democrats* (1905), https://www.marxists.org/archive/hyndman/1905/07/state.htm.
23. Mike Taber, *Under the Banner of Socialism: Resolutions of the Second International, 1889–1912* (Chicago: Haymarket Books, 2021), 4.
24. Ibid., 40.
25. Thane, "The Working Class and State 'Welfare' in Britain, 1880–1914," 884.
26. Noel Whiteside, "Social Welfare and Industrial Relations 1914–1939," in *A History of British Industrial Relations 1914–1939*, ed. Chris Wrigley (Aldershot: Gregg Revivals, 1993), 214.
27. Thane, "The Working Class and State 'Welfare' in Britain, 1880–1914," 885.

28. Stuart Macintyre, *A Proletarian Science: Marxism in Britain, 1917–1933* (London: Lawrence and Wishart, 1986), 177–78.

29. Pat Thane, "The Labour Party and State 'Welfare,'" in *The First Labour Party 1906–1914*, ed. Kenneth D. Brown (London: Routledge, 1985).

30. Cronin and Weiler, "Working-Class Interests and the Politics of Social Democratic Reform in Britain, 1900–1940," 51.

31. Bently B. Gilbert, *British Social Policy 1914–1919* (London: B. T. Batsford, 1970), 28–29.

32. Whiteside, "Social Welfare and Industrial Relations 1914–1939," 216.

33. Ralph Miliband, *Parliamentary Socialism: A Study in the Politics of Labour* (Oxford: Merlin Press, 2009), 59–60.

34. Jane Morgan, *Conflict and Order: The Police and Labour Disputes in England and Wales* (Oxford: Clarendon Press, 1987), 21.

35. Miliband, *Parliamentary Socialism: A Study in the Politics of Labour,* 59.

36. John Saville, "The Welfare State: An Historical Approach," *The New Reasoner* 3 (1957–58): 12–13.

37. Macintyre, *A Proletarian Science: Marxism in Britain, 1917–1933,* 195.

38. Vicente Navarro, *Crisis, Health, and Medicine: A Social Critique* (New York: Tavistock Publications, 1986), 47.

39. Third Congress of the Communist International, *On Tactics,* 12 July 1921 (drafted by Russian delegation in consultation with German delegation; introduced by Radek), https://www.marxists.org/history/international/comintern/3rd-congress/tactics.htm.

40. Whiteside, "Social Welfare and Industrial Relations 1914–1939," 220–21.

41. Noreen Branson, *George Lansbury and the Councillor's Revolt: Poplarism, 1919–1925* (London: Lawrence and Wishart, 1979), 20.

42. Alan Johnson, "The Political Leadership of Popularism," in eds., *Class Struggle and Social Welfare,* ed. Michael Lavalette and Gerry Mooney (London: Routledge, 2000), 101.

43. P. A. Ryan, "'Popularism' 1894–1930," in *The Origins of British Social Policy,* ed. Pat Thane (London: Croom Helm, 1978).

44. Taber, *Under the Banner of Socialism: Resolutions of the Second International, 1889–1912,* 76.

45. Whiteside, "Social Welfare and Industrial Relations 1914–1939," 224.

6. Social Security

1. Norman Ginsburg, *Class, Capital and Social Policy* (London: Macmillan, 1979), 47.

2. Frederick Engels, *The Origin of the Family, Private Property, and the State* (New York: Pathfinder Press, 1976), 160.

3. See David Matthews, "The Working-Class Struggle for Welfare in

Britain," *Monthly Review* 69, no. 9 (February 2018), for an overview of the extent to which the working class in Britain fought for and influenced the evolution of welfare provisions.

4. James O'Connor, *The Fiscal Crisis of the State* (New York: St. Martin's Press, 1973), 6–7.
5. Karl Marx, *Capital*, vol. 1 (London: Lawrence and Wishart, 1977), 600–603.
6. Fred Magdoff and Harry Magdoff, "Disposable Workers: Today's Reserve Army of Labor," *Monthly Review* 55, no.11 (April 2004):18–35.
7. Marx, *Capital*, vol. 1, 601–3.
8. Gov.UK, Benefit Cap, https://www.gov.uk/benefit–cap/benefit–cap-amounts (2022); Steven Kennedy, Wendy Wilson, Vyara Apostolova, Richard Keen, *The Benefit Cap: Briefing Paper 06294* (London: House of Commons Library, November 2016), https://researchbriefings.parliament.uk/ResearchBriefing/Summary/SN06294.
9. Kennedy, Wilson et al., *The Benefit Cap: Briefing Paper 06294*, 8.
10. Claus Offe, *Contradictions of the Welfare State* (Cambridge, MA: MIT Press, 1984), 92–93.
11. Chris Jones and Tony Novak, "The State and Social Policy," in *Capitalism, State Formation and Marxist Theory*, ed. Philip Corrigan (London: Quartet Books, 1980), 153–54.
12. Ibid., 154.
13. David Cameron, *PM's Speech on the Fightback after the Riots* (GOV.UK, 2011), https://www.gov.uk/government/speeches/pms–speech–on–the–fightback–after–the–riots.
14. Department for Work and Pensions, *Universal Credit at Work: Spring 2015*, May 15, 2020, https://assets.publishing.service.gov.uk/media/5a8093d440f0b62305b8bf6b/uc-at-work-spring-2015.pdf.
15. Department for Work and Pensions, *Universal Credit at Work*, 5.
16. Ginsburg, *Class, Capital and Social Policy*, 47.
17. Grover, "New Labour, Welfare Reform and the Reserve Army of Labour," 17–23.
18. Department of Work and Pensions, *Universal Credit Statistics, 29 April 2013 to 14 July 2022*, https://www.gov.uk/government/statistics/universal–credit–statistics–29–april–2013–to–14–july–2022/universal–credit–statistics–29–april–2013–to–14–july–2022#:~:text=There%20were%202.3%20million%20people,periods%20covering%209%20June%202022.
19. Department for Work and Pensions, *Universal Credit at Work: December 2015*, May 15, 2020, https://assets.publishing.service.gov.uk/media/5a750ebc40f0b6397f35d551/universal-credit-at-work -december-2015.pdf.

20. V. I. Lenin, The Sixth (Prague) All-Russia Conference of the R.S.D.L.P. https://www.marxists.org/archive/lenin/works/1912/6thconf/pawsidb. htm.

21. Ibid.

22. Mike Taber, *Under the Banner of Socialism: Resolutions of the Second International, 1889–1912* (Chicago: Haymarket Books, 2021), 40.

23. Eric Hobsbawm, *The Age of Extremes: The Short Twentieth Century 1914–1991* (London: Abucus, 1995), 88–89.

24. Bently B. Gilbert, *British Social Policy 1914–1919* (London: B. T. Batsford, 1970), 66.

25. Ibid., 218.

26. Jason Annetts, Alex Law, Wallace McNeish and Gerry Mooney, *Understanding Social Welfare Movements* (Bristol: Policy Press, 2009), 105.

27. Tony Novak, *Poverty and the State* (Milton Keynes: Open University Press, 1988), 167–68.

28. Ellen Clifford, *The War on Disabled People: Capitalism, Welfare and the Making of a Human Catastrophe* (London: Zed Books, 2020), 2.

29. Bob Williams-Findlay, "The Disabled People's Movement in the Age of Austerity: Rights, Resistance and Reclamation," in *Resist the Punitive State: Grassroots Struggles across Welfare, Housing, Education and Prisons*, ed. Emily Luise Hart, Joe Greener, and Rich Moth (London: Pluto Press, 2020), 136.

30. Ibid., 141.

31. Clifford, *The War on Disabled People: Capitalism, Welfare and the Making of a Human Catastrophe,* 290.

32. Sean Damer, "State, Class and Housing: Glasgow 1885–1919," in *Housing, Social Policy and the State*, ed. Joseph Melling (London: Croom Helm, 1980), 74.

33. Jennifer Dale, "Class Struggle, Social Policy and State Structure: Central-Local Relations and Housing Policy, 1919–1939," in Melling, ed., *Housing, Social Policy and the State*, 197.

34. Karl Marx, *Capital*, vol. 3 (London: Lawrence and Wishart, 1971), 440.

35. Michael Lebowitz, *Between Capitalism and Community* (New York: Monthly Review Press, 2020), 122–24.

7. Disability

1. Institute for Health Metrics and Evaluation, *Findings from the Global Burden of Disease Study 2017* (Seattle: IHME, 2018), 13.

2. World Health Organization, *Disability and Health: Key Facts*, https://www.who.int/news–room/fact–sheets/detail/disability–and–health.

3. Union of the Physically Impaired Against Segregation, *Fundamental*

Principles of Disability (London: Union of the Physically Impaired Against Segregation, 1976).

4. Michael Oliver and Colin Barnes, *The New Politics of Disablement* (Basingstoke: Palgrave Macmillan, 2012), 20–22.
5. Marta Russell, "Disablement, Oppression, and the Political Economy," *Journal of Disability Policy Studies* 12, no. 2 (2001): 87–95.
6. Karl Marx, *Capital*, vol. 1 (London: Lawrence and Wishart, 1977), 173–75.
7. Ibid., 395.
8. Ibid., 397.
9. Ibid., 398.
10. Ibid., 380.
11. Ibid.
12. Russell, "Disablement, Oppression, and the Political Economy," 88.
13. Karl Marx, *Capital*, vol. 3 (London: Lawrence and Wishart, 1972), 88.
14. Frederick Engels, *The Condition of the Working Class in England* (Oxford: Oxford University Press, 2009).
15. Engels, *The Condition of the Working Class in England*, 172–73.
16. Engels, *The Condition of the Working Class in England*, 173.
17. Marx, *Capital*, vol. 1, 602–3.
18. Ibid., 603.
19. Andrew Powell, *Disabled People in Employment: Briefing Paper, Number 7540*, 18 March 2024, https://researchbriefings.files.parliament.uk/documents/CBP-7540/CBP-7540.pdf
20. Adam Tinson, Hannah Aldridge, Theo Barry Born, and Ceri Hughes, *Disability and Poverty: Why Disability Must Be at the Centre of Poverty Reduction* (London: New Policy Institute, 2016), https://www.npi.org.uk/publications/income–and–poverty/disability–and–poverty/.
21. Brigid Francis-Devine, *Poverty in the UK: Statistics Briefing Paper, Number 7096*, 8 April 2024, https://researchbriefings.files.parliament.uk/documents/SN07096/SN07096.pdf.
22. Deborah Stone, *The Disabled State* (Philadelphia: Temple University Press, 1984), 172.
23. Ibid., 172–73.
24. Ibid., 118.
25. Ibid., 180.
26. Ibid., 27.
27. Chris Grover and Linda Piggott, "Disabled People, the Reserve Army of Labour and Welfare Reform," *Disability and Society* 20, no.7 (2005): 710.
28. Marx, *Capital*, vol. 1, 592.
29. Ibid., 598.

30. Ibid., 596.
31. Fred Magdoff and Harry Magdoff, "Disposable Workers: Today's Reserve Army of Labor," *Monthly Review* 55, no.11 (April 2004): 18–35.
32. Mark Hyde, "From Welfare to Work? Social Policy for Disabled People of Working Age in the United Kingdom in the 1990s," *Disability and Society* 15, no. 2 (2000): 336.
33. Grover and Piggott, *Disabled People, the Reserve Army of Labour and Welfare Reform*, 711.
34. Ellen Clifford, *The War on Disabled People: Capitalism, Welfare and the Making of a Human Catastrophe* (London: Zed Books, 2020), 65–66.
35. Grover and Piggott, *Disabled People, the Reserve Army of Labour and Welfare Reform*, 712.
36. ESA constitutes one of the two main disability social policies currently in Britain for working age disabled individuals. The other is Personal Independence Payment (PIP), a non-means-tested benefit. Infused with biomedical understandings of disability, PIP evaluates an individual's functional abilities to assess whether he or she requires financial support to achieve a degree of independent living.
37. Chris Grover and Karen Soldatic, "Neoliberal Restructuring, Disabled People and Social (In)security in Australia and Britain," *Scandinavian Journal of Disability Research* 15, no. 3 (2013): 220.
38. Steven Kennedy, *Incapacity Benefit Reassessment,* House of Commons Library (2014), https://researchbriefings.parliament.uk/ResearchBriefing/Summary/SN06855#fullreport.
39. Steven Kennedy, Andrew Mackley, Roderick McInnes, Bess Jap, Adam Clark, Michael O'Donnell, Alexander Bellis, *Ten Years of the Work Capability Assessment,* 18 April 2019 https://researchbriefings.files.parliament.uk/documents/CDP-2019-0092/CDP-2019-0092.pdf.
40. Marx, *Capital*, vol. 1, 596.
41. Clifford, *The War on Disabled People*, 65–66.
42. Ibid., 2.
43. Matthias Reiss, *Blind Workers Against Charity: The National League of the Blind of Great Britain and Ireland, 1893–1970* (Basingstoke: Palgrave, 2015), 48.
44. Ibid., 48
45. Marta Russell, "What Disability Civil Rights Cannot Do: Employment and Political Economy," *Disability and Society* 17, no.2 (2002): 117–35; Oliver and Barnes, *The New Politics of Disablement*, 143–60.
46. Oliver and Barnes, *The New Politics of Disablement*, 156.
47. Russell, "What Disability Civil Rights Cannot Do," 121.
48. Roddy Slorach, *A Very Capitalist Condition: A History and Politics of Disability* (London: Bookmarks, 2016), 269.

49. Ibid.

8. Health

1.   Karl Marx, *Capital*, vol. 1 (London: Lawrence and Wishart, 1977), 401.
2.   Ibid., 603.
3.   Friedrich Engels, *The Condition of the Working Class in England* (Oxford: Oxford University Press, 2009), 107.
4.   Ibid..
5.   Ibid.
6.   Ibid., 109.
7.   Ibid., 108.
8.   Howard Waitzkin, Alina Perez, Matthew Anderson, *Social Medicine and the Coming Transformation* (London: Routledge, 2021), 24.
9.   Leonard Rodberg and Gelvin Stevenson, "The Healthcare Industry in Advanced Capitalism," *Review of Radical Political Economics* 9, no 1. (1977): 112.
10. Lesley Doyal, *The Political Economy of Health* (London: Pluto Press, 1985), 39.
11. Marx, *Capital*, vol 1, 372
12. Vicente Navarro, *Medicine under Capitalism* (London: Croom Helm, 1976), 215.
13. Since 1999, with the implementation of devolution, establishing the Welsh and Scottish Parliaments, and Northern Irish Assembly, control over healthcare and the creation of health policy has been a devolved issue, resulting in variations between the NHS within all four countries of the UK.
14. NHS England, *The NHS Long-Term Plan*, (2019), 116, https://www.longtermplan.nhs.uk/wp-content/uploads/2019/08/nhs-long-term-plan-version-1.2.pdf.
15. Howard Waitzkin, *The Second Sickness: Contradictions of Capitalist Health Care* (Lanham, MD: Rowman & Littlefield, 2000), 48.
16. Rodberg and Stevenson, *The Healthcare Industry in Advanced Capitalism,*113.
17. Waitzkin, *The Second Sickness: Contradictions of Capitalist Health Care*, 48.
18. Doyal, *The Political Economy of Health*, 34.
19. Navarro, *Medicine under Capitalism*, 126.
20. Lee Humber, *Vital Signs: The Deadly Costs of Health Inequality* (London: Pluto Press: 2019), 14.
21. Britain, UK Parliament, *Health and Social Care Act 2012*, adopted March 2012, sec 1, http://legislation.gov.uk.
22. Allyson Pollock and David Price, *Duty to Care: In Defence of Universal Health Care* (London: Centre for Labour and Social Studies, 2013), 12.

23. *Health and Social Care Act 2012*, sec 1.
24. Allyson Pollock, "Morality and Values in Support of Universal Healthcare Must be Enshrined in Law," *International Journal of Health Policy Management*, 4, no. 6 (2015): 399–402.
25. Roy Hattersley, *David Lloyd George: The Great Outsider* (London: Little Brown, 2010), 299.
26. Vicente Navarro, *Class Struggle, the State, and Medicine: An Historical and Contemporary Analysis of the Medical Sector in Great Britain* (Los Gatos, CA: Robertson, 1978), 10.
27. Mike Taber, *Under the Socialist Banner: Resolutions of the Second International, 1889–1912* (Chicago: Haymarket, 2021), 76.
28. Navarro, *Class Struggle, the State, and Medicine: An Historical and Contemporary Analysis of the Medical Sector in Great Britain*, 15.
29. Communist Party of Great Britain, *Draft Programme of the C.P.G.B. to the Comintern*, https://www.marxists.org/history/international/comintern/sections/britain/periodicals/communist_review/1924/02/draft_programme.htm.
30. David Stark Murray, *Why a National Health Service? The Part Played by the Socialist Medical Association* (London: Pemberton Books, 1971).
31. John Stewart, "For a Healthy London: The Socialist Medical Association and the London County Council in the 1930s," *Medical History* 41, no 4. (October 1997): 435.
32. Brian Barker, *Labour in London* (London: George Routledge and Sons, 1946).
33. Stewart, "For a Healthy London," 427–28.
34. Navarro, *Class Struggle, the State, and Medicine: An Historical and Contemporary Analysis of the Medical Sector in Great Britain*, 33.
35. Aneurin Bevan, *In Place of Fear* (New York: Simon and Schuster, 1952), 86.
36. Michael Savage, "Public Support for Nurses' Strike Piles Pressure on Sunak and Divides Tories," *The Guardian*, December 17, 2022, https://www.theguardian.com/uk-news/2022/dec/17/public-support-nurses-strike-pressure-sunak-tories.
37. For more on the development of healthcare in Wales between 1999 and 2020, see David Matthews, "Health Policy in Wales: Two Decades of Devolution," in *Social Policy for Welfare Practice in Wales*, 3rd ed., ed. Hefin Gwilym and Charlotte Williams (Birmingham: British Association of Social Workers, 2021), 67–80.

9. Housing

1. Karl Marx, *Capital*, vol. 1 (London: Lawrence and Wishart, 1977), 615.
2. Ibid., 619.

3. David Harvey, *The Limits to Capital* (London: Verso, 2006), 224–38.
4. David Harvey, *The New Imperialism* (Oxford: Oxford University Press, 2003), 100.
5. Marx, *Capital,* vol. 1, 615–16.
6. Ibid., 617.
7. Michael Berry, "Posing the Housing Question in Australia: Elements of a Theoretical Framework for a Marxist Analysis of Housing," *Antipode* 13, no.1 (1981): 4.
8. David Madden and Peter Marcuse, *In Defense of Housing* (London: Verso, 2016), 26.
9. Michael Harloe, *The People's Home? Social Rented Housing in Europe & America* (Oxford: Blackwell, 1995), 2.
10. David Harvey, "The Art of Rent: Globalization, Monopoly and the Commodification of Culture," *Socialist Register: A World of Contradictions* (2002): 97.
11. Berry, *Posing the Housing Question in Australia: Elements of a Theoretical Framework for a Marxist Analysis of Housing*, 6.
12. Ibid., 6.
13. Keith Bassett and John Short, *Housing and Residential Structure: Alternative Approaches* (London: Routledge and Kegan Paul, 1980), 210.
14. David Harvey, *Seventeen Contradictions and the End of Capitalism* (London: Profile Books, 2014), 41.
15. Tithi Bhattacharya, "Liberating Women from Political Economy: Margaret Benston's Marxism as a Social Reproduction Approach to Gender Oppression," *Monthly Review* 71, no. 8 (January 2020): 11.
16. Berry, *Posing the Housing Question in Australia: Elements of a Theoretical Framework for a Marxist Analysis of Housing*, 6.
17. Michael E. Stone, "Housing, Mortgage Lending, and the Contradictions of Capitalism," in *Marxism and the Metropolis: New Perspectives in Urban Political Economy,* ed. William K. Tabb and Larry Sawers (New York: Oxford University Press, 1978), 183–85.
18. Paul Baran and Paul Sweezy, *Monopoly Capital: An Essay on the American Economic and Social Order* (New York: Monthly Review Press, 1966), 299.
19. Norman Ginsburg, *Class, Capital and Social Policy* (Basingstoke: Macmillan, 1979), 108–9.
20. Caroline Beale "Property Relations and Housing Policy: Oldham in the Late Nineteenth and Early Twentieth Centuries," in *Housing, Social Policy and the State,* ed. Joseph Melling (London: Croom Helm, 1980), 41.
21. Ginsburg, *Class, Capital and Social Policy,* 140–41.

22. Sean Damer "State, Class and Housing: Glasgow 1885–1919," in Melling, ed. *Housing, Social Policy and the State*, 78–79.
23. Ginsburg, *Class, Capital and Social Policy,* 140–41.
24. Damer, "State, Class and Housing: Glasgow 1885–1919," 79.
25. Ginsburg, *Class, Capital and Social Policy,* 141.
26. John Boughton, *Municipal Dreams: The Rise and Fall of Council Housing* (London: Verso, 2019), 16–17.
27. Ibid., 30.
28. David Renton, "Housing: As It Is, and As It Might Be," *International Socialism*, 2012, 134, https://isj.org.uk/housing-as-it-is-and-as-it-might-be/.
29. Sean Damer. "The Clyde Rent War! The Clydebank Rent Strike of the 1920s," in *Class Struggle and Social Welfare*, ed. Michael Lavalette and Gerry Mooney (London: Routledge, 2000), 73.
30. Sean Damer, "The Clyde Rent War! The Clydebank Rent Strike of the 1920s," 73.
31. Damer, "State, Class and Housing: Glasgow 1885–1919," 103.
32. Damer, "The Clyde Rent War! The Clydebank Rent Strike of the 1920s," 93
33. Keith Middlemas, *The Clydesiders* (London: Hutchinson, 1965), 151.
34. Communist Party of Great Britain, *Draft Programme of the C.P.G.B to the Comintern* (1924), https://www.marxists.org/history/international/comintern/sections/britain/periodicals/communist_review/1924/02/draft_programme.htm.
35. Aneurin Bevan, *Housing Bill, March 1949*, https://api.parliament.uk/historic-hansard/commons/1949/mar/16/housing-bill.
36. Calculated from Department for Communities and Local Government, Permanent Dwellings Completed by Tenure, United Kingdom: Historical Calendar Year Series, https://www.gov.uk/government/statistical-data-sets/live-tables-on-house-building.
37. Renton, "Housing: As It Is, and As It Might Be."
38. Communist Party of Great Britain, *The British Road to Socialism* (1951), https://www.marxists.org/history/international/comintern/sections/britain/brs/1951/51.htm.
39. David Matthews, "The Struggle for Shelter: Class Conflict and Public Housing in Britain," *Monthly Review* 69, no. 4 (September 2017): 48.
40. Renton, "Housing: As It Is, and As It Might Be."
41. Defend Council Housing, "A Manifesto for Council Housing," March 2010, http://defendcouncilhousing.org.
42. Social Housing Action Group, "Policy Discission Paper: Top Ten Demands for the Labour Party," December 2018, https://shaction.org/policy-papers/.
43. Office for National Statistics, "House Building, UK: Permanent

Dwellings Started and Completed by County," May 2023, https://www.ons.gov.uk/peoplepopulationandcommunity/housing/datasets/ukhousebuildingpermanentdwellingsstartedandcompleted.

10. Education

1. Karl Marx and Frederick Engels, *The Communist Manifesto* (London: Penguin, 1985), 105.
2. Frederick Engels, *The Principles of Communism*, Marxist Internet Archive, https://www.marxists.org/archive/marx/works/1847/11/princom.htm.
3. Robin Small, *Marx and Education* (Aldershot: Ashgate, 2005), viii.
4. Brian Simon, "Marx and the Crisis in Education," *Marxism Today* 21, no. 7 (1977); Glenn Rikowski, "Marx and the Education of the Future," *Policy Future in Education* 2, nos. 3 and 4 (2004).
5. Karl Marx, *Critique of the Gotha Programme* (1875), https://www.marxists.org/archive/marx/works/1875/gotha/ch04.htm.
6. Simon, *Marx and the Crisis in Education*, 198.
7. Karl Marx, *The International Workingmen's Association* (1866), Marxist Internet Archive, https://www.marxists.org/history/international/iwma/documents/1866/instructions.htm#04.
8. Ibid.
9. Karl Marx, *Capital*, vol. 1 (London: Lawrence and Wishart, 1977), 454.
10. V. I. Lenin, *The Agrarian Programme of Social Democracy in the First Russian Revolution, 1905–1907*, https://www.marxists.org/archive/lenin/works /1907/agrprogr/index.htm.
11. Nikolai Bukharin and Evgenii Preobrazhensky, *The ABC of Communism* (Pattern Books, 2021), 227. It has not been possible to locate the place of publication.
12. Louis Althusser, *Lenin and Philosophy and Other Essays* (London: NLB, 1977), 126.
13. Madan Sarup, *Marxism and Education* (London: Routledge & Kegan Paul, 1978), 140.
14. Samuel Bowles and Herbert Gintis, *Schooling in Capitalist America: Educational Reform and the Contradiction of Economic Life* (London: Routledge and Kegan Paul, 1976).
15. Ibid., 126.
16. Ibid., 125.
17. Ibid., 126.
18. Ibid., 130.
19. Ibid., 131.
20. Madan Sarup, *Education, State and Crisis: A Marxist Perspective* (London: Routledge & Kegan Paul, 1982), 41–42.

21. Confederation of British Industry, *Education and Learning for the Modern World: CBI/Pearson Education and Skills Survey Report 2019* (2019), https://www.cbi.org.uk/media/3841/12546_tess_2019.pdf.

22. Bukharin and Preobrazhensky, *The ABC of Communism*, 227.

23. Rachel Sharp, *Knowledge, Ideology and the Politics of Schooling: Towards a Marxist Analysis of Education* (London: Routledge & Kegan Paul, 1980), 116.

24. Louis Althusser, *Lenin and Philosophy and Other Essays*, 127.

25. Michael Apple, *Ideology and Curriculum* (London: Routledge & Keegan Paul, 1982), 14.

26. Althusser, *Lenin and Philosophy and Other Essays*, 147.

27. Sharp, *Knowledge, Ideology and the Politics of Schooling: Towards a Marxist Analysis of Education*, 124.

28. Apple, *Ideology and Curriculum*, 63.

29. Bowles and Gintis, *Schooling in Capitalist America: Educational Reform and the Contradiction of Economic Life*, 236.

30. Ibid., 238.

31. Ibid., 12.

32. Ibid., 12.

33. Ibid., 239–40.

34. Ibid., 240.

35. Sidney Webb, *Twentieth-Century Politics: A Policy of National Efficiency* (London: Fabian Society, 1901).

36. Richard Johnson, "'Really Useful Knowledge': Radical Education and Working-Class Culture, 1790-1848," in John Clarke, Chas Critcher, and Richard Johnson, eds., *Working Class Culture: Studies in History and Theory* (London: Hutchinson & Co, 1979), 75–80.

37. Ibid., 94–95.

38. Simon, *Education and the Labour Movement, 1870–1920*, 128–30.

39. Ibid., 156.

40. David Rubinstein and Brian Simon, *The Evolution of the Comprehensive School: 1926–1966* (London, Routledge & Kegan Paul, 1969), 1.

41. Communist Party of Great Britain, *Draft Programme of the C.P.G.B to the Comintern* (1924), https://www.marxists.org/history/international/comintern/sections/britain/periodicals/communist_review/1924/02/draft_programme.htm.

42. Communist Party of Great Britain, *Britain's Road to Socialism* (1951), https://www.marxists.org/history/international/comintern/sections/britain/brs/1951/51.htm.

43. Anthony Crossland, *Socialism Now and Other Essays* (London: Jonathan Cape, 1974), 204.

44. Stephen J. Ball, "The Legacy of ERA, Privatization and the Policy

Ratchet," *Educational Management Administration & Leadership* 36, no. 2 (2008).

45. John Fitz and Thaker Hafid, "Perspectives on the Privatization of Public Schooling in England and Wales," *Educational Policy* 21, no. 1 (2007).

46. National Education Union, *The NEU Case Against Academisation* (2022), https://neu.org.uk/policy/neu-case-against-academisation.

11. A Radical Alternative for a Progressive Future

1. V. I. Lenin, "The State and Revolution," in *Essential Works of Lenin*, ed. Henry M. Christman (New York: Dover Publications, 1987), 398.

2. Che Guevara, "Socialism and Man in Cuba," in *Che Guevara Reader: Writings on Guerrilla Strategy, Politics and Revolution*, ed, David Deutschman (Melbourne: Ocean Press, 1997), 211.

3. Adreas Chatzidakis, Jamie Hakim, Jo Littler, Catherine Rottenberg, Lynne Segal, *The Care Manifesto: The Politics of Interdependence* (London: Verso, 2020), 2–4.

4. Erik Olin Wright, *How to Be an Anticapitalist in the Twenty-First Century* (London: Verso, 2021), 18.

5. Guevara, "Socialism and Man in Cuba," 205.

6. Richard Titmuss, *A Commitment to Welfare* (Bristol: Bristol University Press, 2020), 116.

7. Richard Titmuss, "Goals of Today's Welfare State," in *Towards Socialism*, ed. Perry Anderson and Robin Blackburn (London: Fontana Library, 1965), 355–56.

8. Karl Marx, *Capital,* vol. 3 (London: Lawrence and Wishart, 1971), 440.

9. International Workers of the World (IWW), https://iww.org.uk/preamble/.

10. The Symbiosis Research Collective, "How to build a new world in the shell of the old." *Ecologist*, 23rd April 2018, https://theecologist.org/2018/apr/23/how-build-new-world-shell-old.

11. Michael Lebowitz, *Between Capitalism and Community* (New York: Monthly Review Press, 2020), 122–24.

12. Peter Kropotkin, *Modern Science and Anarchy* (1908), https://theanarchistlibrary.org/library/petr-kropotkin-modern-science-and-anarchy.

13. Pandemic Reserarch for the People, *Moving Beyond Capitalist Agriculture: Could Agroecology Prevent Further Pandemics?* (2021), https://mronline.org/2021/08/01/moving-beyond-capitalist-agriculture-could-agroecology-prevent-further-pandemics/.

14. Colin Ward, *Social Policy: An Anarchist Response* (London: Freedom Press, 1996), 11.

15. George Ciccariello-Maher, *Building the Commune: Radical Democracy in Venezuela* (London: Verso, 2016).

16. Joel Izlar, "Radical Social Welfare and Anti-Authoritarian Mutual Aid," *Critical and Radical Social Work* 7, no. 3 (2019): 349–66.

17. Emma Goldman, "The Individual, Society and the State," in *Red Emma Speaks: An Emma Goldman Reader*, ed. Alix Kates Shulman (Amherst: Humanity Books, 1998).

18. Titmuss, *A Commitment to Welfare*, 161.

19. Ibid., 135.

20. Erik Olin Wright, *How to Be an Anticapitalist in the Twenty-First Century*, 103.

Index

of, 39–41; labor struggles and, 41–47; Marxist theory on, 57; progressive systems for, 190–94; as social control, 82–84; supported by British unions, 98

welfare reforms: in Britain, 77–79; disabled labor force and, 125–28; labor movement and, 90–92; National League of the Blind and, 128–32; Second International on, 89–90; working class opposition to, 85–89

welfare state: British working class hostility toward, 85–87; within capitalist state, 34–36; class struggle and, 43–47; development of, in Britain, 72–73; as dialectical object, 42–43; disabilities under, 117, 122, 123; emergence of, 17–18; ideological role of, 40–41; labor and, 15–17; Marxist analyses of, 13–15, 38–39; working class in development of, 182–83

West Ham (East London), 157
Wheatley, John, 159–60
Wheatley Housing Act (Britain, 1924), 159–60
Williams-Findlay, Bob, 112
women: employment of, 138; Factory Act on, 60–61
Work Capability Assessment (WCA), 125–27

Workers' Socialist Federation (Britain), 94

workfare, 112–13

working class: in development of welfare state, 44–45, 182–83; growth and decline of, in Britain, 73–75; health of, 135–36; hostility to welfare state among, 85–86; housing in reproduction of, 155–56; Marx and Engels on housing of, 149–52; poverty among, in late nineteenth-century Britain, 80–81; struggles for healthcare by, 143–45; welfare reforms and, 77–78

working day: class struggle and, 60–65; eight-hour day, 16; 10 Hours Bill on, 58–60

Workmen's National Housing Council (WNHC; Britain), 157–58

Work-Related Activity Group, 126–28

Wright, Erik Olin: on capitalist states, 33–34; on community, 186; on reforms under capitalism, 48; on social democratic reforms, 55; on welfare under capitalism, 198

Yates, Michael D., 16, 55

www.ingramcontent.com/pod-product-compliance
Ingram Content Group UK Ltd.
Pitfield, Milton Keynes, MK11 3LW, UK
UKHW042235060325
455777UK00005B/48